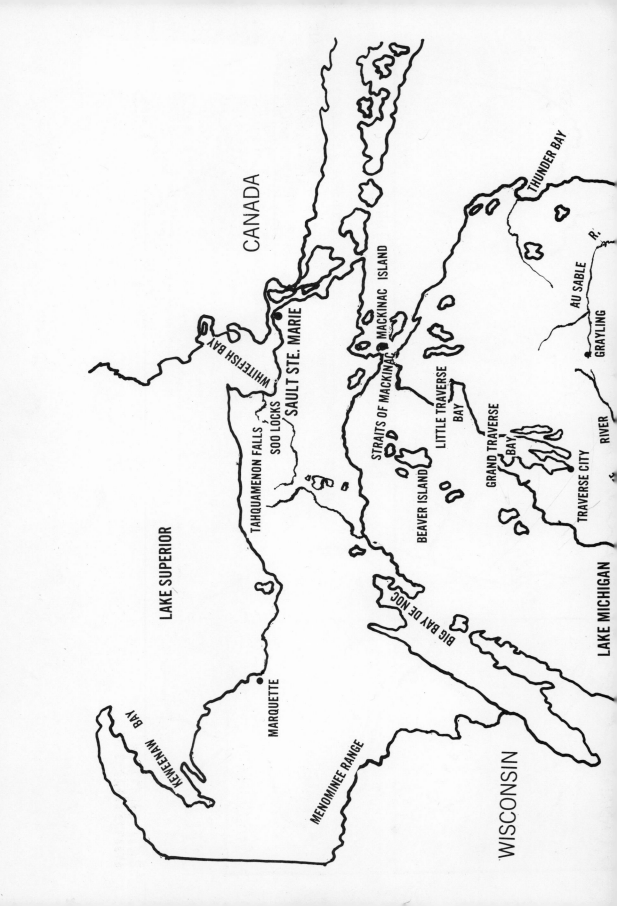

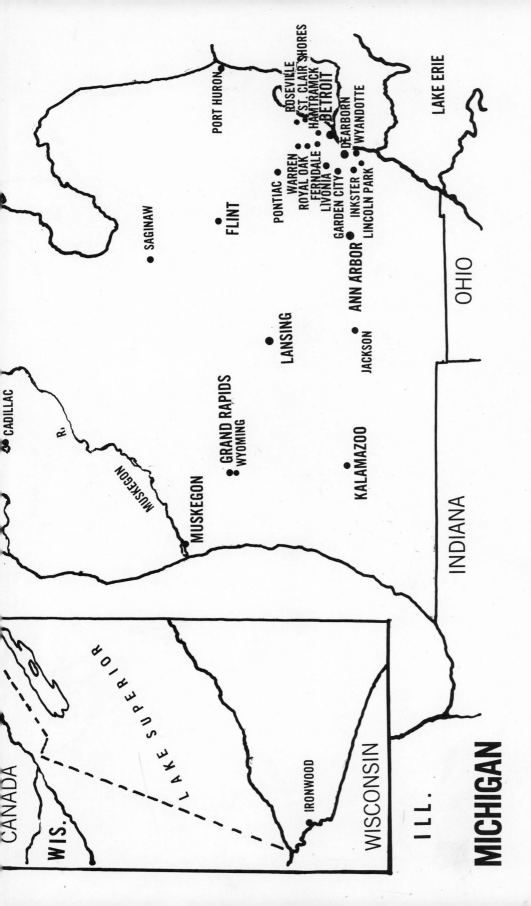

MICHIGAN

26th
State to join the Union

RIVER ROUGE PLANT
APPLE BLOSSOM
STATE FLAG
HENRY FORD I

MICHIGAN

by Russel B. Nye

Michigan has many contrasting faces—teeming industrial cities like Detroit, the automobile empire of the world; rich fruit and dairy farms; bustling seaports where freighters from all over the world steam in and out through the St. Lawrence Seaway and the Great Lakes; and the quiet beauty of the northern peninsula with rivers, lakes and forest offering hunting, fishing and magnificent scenery to the visitor and sportsman alike.

Russel Nye presents a vivid picture of his home state through geography, history, industry, people and recreation. He explores what Michigan is today and how it came about. He takes the reader back to the early days when Indian, Frenchman, and Englishman vied for Michigan's abundance of natural resources, to Michigan's emergence as a state of the Union, through the development of shipping on the Great Lakes, the rise of the automobile industry in Detroit, to present-day Michigan which is a state which *makes* things—from canned cherries and breakfast cereal to diesel trucks and rocket launchers.

MI

CONSULTANT: Mildred Nickel
Director of School Libraries, Lansing School District

STATES OF THE NATION

CHIGAN

by Russel B. Nye

COWARD-McCANN, INC.

PHOTO CREDITS

American Forest Products Industries, pages 26-27, 67, 71
Automobile Manufacturers Association, pages 78, 81, 82, 84, 85
City of Detroit, Department of Report and Information Committee, page 77
Detroit Edison Company, pages 12, 15, 19, 31, 45, 74, 86
Dossin Great Lakes Museum, pages 51, 52-53, 56
East Michigan Tourist Association, title page, 94, 99, 112-113
Ford Motor Company, Educational Affairs Department, 80
Michigan Bell Telephone Company, pages 36-37, 38, 46-47, 55, 64, 72, 102-103, 108-109
Michigan Department of Conservation, pages 7, 24, 28, 29, 68, 69
Michigan State University, Department of Information Services, page 89
Michigan Tourist Council, pages 8, 9, 10-11, 14, 21, 22, 40-41, 44, 57, 60, 63, 92-93
Southeastern Michigan Tourist Association, page 75
University of Michigan, page 32
West Michigan Tourist Association, pages 23, 43

Jacket
River Rouge Plant, Ford Motor Company, *Ewing Galloway*
Apple Blossom, *Bollenbacher*
Michigan state flag, *Reprinted with permission of the copyright owner, F. E. Compton Co., division of Encyclopaedia Britannica, Inc., Chicago, Illinois*
Henry Ford I, *Courtesy Educational Affairs Department, Ford Motor Company*
Maps, Bob Gray

Library of Congress Catalog Card Number: AC 65-20394
PRINTED IN THE UNITED STATES OF AMERICA
082012

CONTENTS

Chapter 1

Chapter 2

Chapter 3

Chapter 4

Chapter 5

Chapter 6

Chapter 7

Chapter 8

Chapter 9

Chapter 1

Michigan: A First Look

Michigan shows many faces to the world. It is a land of long distances and wide landscapes, of cities and farms, of water and woods. It is familiar in its daily ways to those who know the typical face of Midwestern America.

Michigan is made up of an upper and a lower peninsula. The Lower Peninsula, shaped like a mitten pointing up from the Great Lakes toward Canada, marks the beginning boundary of the Midwest. Like its sister Lake states, Michigan is rich, big, and varied. Connecticut, Massachusetts and Rhode Island could all be fitted into the Upper Peninsula alone, with space left over. It is farther from Detroit, in the southern section of the Lower Peninsula, to Ironwood, in the Upper Peninsula, than it is from New York City to Detroit. This expansiveness is part of the Midwest's character, and part of the face that Michigan turns to the visitor.

6

Michigan woods in winter

To one who enters Michigan from Ohio or Indiana there is no obvious change. The flat, rich lake plains stretch away to the horizon, rolling a bit here and there, just as they do near Wauseon, Ohio, or South Bend, Indiana. Toward the west, the damp Michigan marshlands give way to the fertile, blackish "prairie" lands that the settlers found so attractive in the Battle Creek, Kalamazoo, and Three Rivers area. And again the land changes near the lake's edge to the light soil of the great sandy belt that runs from the foot of Lake Michigan north to the Straits of Mackinac, which divide the Lower Peninsula from the Upper Peninsula. The southern half of Michigan, where almost three-quarters of its population lives, is recognizably Midwestern.

Michigan *is* the Midwest, of course, in temper, thought, and geography. But it is the North, too. Start toward the Straits of Mackinac on any of the great north-south arteries of travel — and something happens. The traveler drives for miles through pleasant green farm-

Plains farm in Lower Peninsula

lands without noticing the subtle changes around him. Suddenly, somewhere near Reed City, or Clare, or West Branch, he is in the North — the land, the forests, the light of day and the stars at night have a Northern feel. The birch and pines lean differently in the clear air; blue scraps of water sparkle now and then from tangled acres of trees and brush. No one can quite identify the point where it occurs, or the exact reason for it, but Midwestern Michigan has disappeared and Northern Michigan has come in its place. Crossing the sparkling waters of the Straits of Mackinac emphasizes the change. The Upper Peninsula is a truly Northern land of dark green distances, of deer that dart back into the trees as you pass, of icy clear winters with deep snows, and brief, cool, incredibly brown-and-gold autumn days. No one who has been north of Clare can doubt that Michigan is the North, as well as the Midwest.

This is not all. The traveler through Michigan sees farmland and

Northern Michigan

Lake Superior

woods, village and town; yet no matter where he is, he is only a few miles away from the Great Lakes, four of which Lake Superior, Lake Michigan, Lake Huron, and Lake Erie surround Michigan with a deep blue ring and isolate it from its neighbors. Nowhere in Michigan is one more than eighty-five miles from one of the Lakes. It is easy to forget, driving up the spine of the state, that Michigan is a maritime state, with more than three thousand miles of coastline and a hundred ports. You remember it, though, at places like Port Huron, or Muskegon, or Alpena, or Marquette, or Ludington, or most of all at the Soo Canal on the Upper Peninsula, where the shipping tonnage that passes through each year exceeds that of the Thames, the Rhine, the Volga, the Danube, and the Seine rivers combined. Less than two hours' drive

from quiet dairy farms in western Michigan, the gulls caw and wheel over the long lakeboats that slide by the coastline on to Gary, Indiana, or Milwaukee, Wisconsin, or perhaps to Europe. A few miles from family summer cottages on Burt Lake, the smoke of ships bound from Duluth, Superior, and Port Arthur lies flat on the sky over Lake Huron. The breeze that blows into Michigan from east, north, and west may not be as salty as Cape Cod's in Massachusetts, but it has its own kind of seafaring taste.

Michigan is, then, both Midwest and North, ship and shore, farm and forest, country and town — and cities. The most spectacular proof of this comes to the visitor who arrives from the East by air, coasting over the wrinkled waters of Lake Erie and the neat parallelograms of

Detroit

farms and roads, until suddenly Detroit explodes underneath him in a welter of smoke stacks, streets, tracks, streams of traffic and colored lights. The traveler who comes by train or automobile feels the impact of the big industrial city, too, not quite so sharply as the air traveler perhaps, but few who have seen the huge bulk of the Ford Rouge plant suddenly loom up ahead forget the experience. This is still another face of Michigan, the face of its cities.

Detroit is king of them all, a sprawling, muscular, teeming place that sucks in coal and iron and steel and rubber and gas and spews out automobiles, trucks, machinery, parts and tools so that the rest of the world can hurry along a little faster on wheels and wings. The other production cities — Flint, Pontiac, Lansing, Saginaw, Grand Rapids, Muskegon, Jackson and the rest — have their own Detroitlike personality, too. It is made up of rivers of men at the factory gates when the shift changes, the white glare from factory windows at night, the subterranean thud of giant presses blocks away, the sad honk of diesel freights in the hours before dawn. Nowhere in southern Michigan, certainly, are you ever very far from a place where something is being made in or for a factory. The farmer may drive to the nearest city to make transmission gears on the second factory shift; the factory worker may drive to his rural home to tend his chickens and his orchard. Farm and factory blend together. The point is, Michigan *makes* things. It makes more automobiles than any other place in the world — and it also, curiously enough, makes bows and arrows, fish lures, magic tricks, guitars, furniture, cereal, gray iron castings, and canned peaches. It makes them in big cities and middle-sized ones and even small ones. Where the factories stand, the cities grow around them, and the suburban towns huddle in close to merge into them.

Beyond the rim of the city there is another flavor to Michigan life. The small town, as much as the city, is a part of the landscape, whether it be buzzing with shoppers and pickup trucks on a Saturday, or dozing in a Wednesday's summer sun in growing season. The pace is different here, slower, more deliberate, careful. People need not hurry, for just beyond the edge of town, a few blocks from the last freshly

Hunting in the Upper Peninsula

painted cottage in the new subdivision, there may be a stream or a patch of woods or a pond where people go in July heat or January cold for picnics or pheasants or a perch or two caught through the ice. Here, in these towns, is the Michigan of the ice-cream social on the church lawn, the city band concert in the park, the Saturday night dance, or the lone hunter, license pinned to his jacket, walking with his dog across a frozen field. This is another face of Michigan which many know.

The people who live in Michigan, of course, know their land and would live nowhere else. The people are as different from each other as the land is different. Some of them love the city, like those Detroiters who feel vaguely uneasy west of the city limits, and to whom the rush-hour din of the main street, Woodward Avenue, is music.

Expressway traffic in Detroit

Others are not really convinced that anything south of the Straits of Mackinac is worth saving. And there are others who feel that a town with more than four traffic lights is too big for relaxed living.

The people are as varied as their state. The Finns, Swedes, French-Canadians, and Welshmen of the Upper Peninsula are as much Michiganders as there are Hamtramck Poles, the Corktown Irish, or the Dutchmen from Holland. These people, and others like them from other lands, give something of their personality and temperament to the places they live and the places they go. New England towns like Marshall, Howell, Dexter, and Vermontville lie among other towns like Clinton, De Witt, Troy, and Onondaga, transplanted from New York State. Frankenmuth and Zeeland reflect their German and Dutch origins; county names like Antrim and Emmet are in memory of an Emerald Isle far away, and Leelanau or Otsego or Gogebic bring

15

to mind the shadows of long-ago red men. St. Ignace and Charlevoix and Alpena could exist only in Michigan's lake country. Ishpeming, Calumet, Escanaba, and Manistique could be only in the Upper Peninsula. There is no single type of Michigan place or person, no "typical Michigander." In Vermont you might identify a Yankee "character," or a "Southern gentleman" in Virginia (as most certainly you could recognize and identify a cowboy in Texas), just as a traveler might find a typical New England crossroads hamlet, a Virginia cotton town, or a Texas cowtown. But not in Michigan. Its people and places are too varied, too swiftly moving for that. Michigan refuses to be typed.

What sort of place, then, is Michigan? What face does it show the world? To answer this is no simple task. It is unlike any other state that lies between the two oceans, shaped and molded by circumstances that prevailed nowhere else and by its own diverse and complicated past and people. No one can quite catch a clear glimpse of its many faces, or draw its picture. It is the slate blue of a lake in summer, the puff of white snow in a winter wood, the gray of city smoke in the dusk,

Atomic power plant near Monroe

the green of farmland, the burst of autumn reds in the hardwood forest. Michigan has more, always, than one has yet seen.

So how do you explain Michigan? How can you describe a state that begins at its southern boundary with a huge industrial empire built on automobiles and ends at its northern tip with vast solitary forests crossed by only a few roads where automobiles can go? How can you explain a state that makes rocket launchers and harpsichords, diesel trucks and canned cherries? What do you say of a state whose recorded history begins before the Pilgrims landed at Plymouth Rock, and whose engineers are now busy making space vehicles?

Rather than trying to explain it, this book takes you on a tour of Michigan, its past, its present, its land and its people. It will be like walking down a long corridor with many doors, opening a few of them to look inside. There will have to be some we pass by, but we can, we hope, discover enough about what the state is like to finish the book with a better idea of how and where Michigan fits into the American pattern.

Chapter 2

The Face of the Land

The earliest travelers in the area heard stories from the Indians of a giant piece of metal, hidden somewhere in the forests. The Indians thought it had been hurled down from the skies by the spirits. Reports agreed that it was probably copper (though some claimed it might be gold) and that only the Ojibwa knew where it was. The Indians verified some of the stories, but since they believed it possessed supernatural powers, they were reluctant to tell any white man where it was. In 1667 they showed it to Father Dablon, a French missionary whom they trusted. He reported that it was the largest piece of copper he had ever seen. A few later travelers reported its existence, and one or two showed chunks of the metal that were so pure and soft that they could be shaped with an ordinary hammer. However, not many travelers penetrated into the Upper Peninsula forests where it lay. Alexander Henry, the English trader, persuaded the Indians to guide

Pentoga park trail

him to the location in 1776. He wrote the first accurate account of it. It was indeed what the reports said — a five-ton piece of such pure metallic copper that Henry chiseled off a hundred-pound piece as a souvenir. It lay ten miles up the Ontonagon River from the edge of Lake Superior.

That the famous Ontonagon Boulder might be a sign of what bounties nature had put under Michigan soil, no one seemed to realize. There it stayed for the next century, hacked and scratched at by the curious, until an alert promoter from Detroit bought it for $150 and hauled it off to the city for exhibition. Finally he lost it to the federal government, which seized it as United States property and put it in the Smithsonian Institution. There it remains, or what is left of it, as a mute reminder of the gifts bestowed on Michigan by time and geology.

The oldest part of Michigan lies in the western end of the Upper Peninsula, where Father Dablon found the Indians' magic copperstone. Here are outcroppings of the Archean layer of rock, the most ancient in the world. These rocks were probably formed when parts of the bottom of the sea that covered Michigan billions of years ago were pushed upward by deep volcanic explosions during the infancy of the very planet itself.

The eastern end of the Upper Peninsula and all the Lower Peninsula are much younger. In early geological time — one or two billion years ago — the whole Great Lakes area formed a huge basin, with a warm, almost tropical climate. Then, about two million years ago, a great ice sheet moved down from Canada, covering Michigan with ice two to four miles thick. This glacier advanced and retreated across Michigan several times, reaching down as far as what is now the Ohio River. Each time the glacier advanced, it gouged out the land like a giant scraper, shearing off the hills, digging up rock and soil, scarring the land with cuts and valleys. All but a few square miles of the surface of Michigan is made up of rock and soil either pushed down from Canada, dug up from below or washed about by melting glacial ice.

The last glacial retreat, which occurred between 10,000 and 35,000 years ago, made Michigan more or less what it looks like today. The

Cedar Creek

melting ice filled up the glacier-dug depressions to make Lakes Michigan, Huron, Erie, and Superior. It also made almost 11,000 smaller lakes, thirty-four river systems, and uncounted hundreds of streams and ponds. The land itself, pressed down by the weight of the great ice sheet, gradually rose up, a few inches at a time, as much as six miles.

Plant life, fish, and animals came. Huge treelike plants, tall ferns and great expanses of marshland covered Michigan. Mammoths, mastodons, musk-oxen, caribou and giant hogs roamed the land. None of them survived, but their fossilized skeletons occasionally are found by road crews and excavators. About one hundred and fifty mastodon skeletons, or parts of them, dating from 8,000 or 10,000 years ago, have been uncovered in Michigan. The most unusual find has been the fossil remains of three whales, one near Flint, another near Oscoda, and a third near Tecumseh. How these adventurous whales ever got to Michigan no one really knows. Geologists think that they swam up the Mississippi River, into the Great Lakes, into the Grand River, and then across into eastern Michigan. It is also possible that one or more of them arrived from the Atlantic via the St. Lawrence River. Wherever they came from, the whales apparently became stranded in the shallow waters of the inland lakes and were buried in the sand.

Michigan is unique among the continental United States in that it is the only state divided by water into two parts, the Upper and Lower Peninsulas. People in Michigan have become accustomed to calling the Upper Peninsula the "U.P.," and the Lower Peninsula simply

Porcupine Mountains

"Michigan." The eastern part of the Upper Peninsula is low and flat, cut by small streams (which have some of the best trout-fishing in the world) and carpeted by marshland and woodland. The western Upper Peninsula is wild and broken forest country, rising up into the rolling Huron and Porcupine Mountains, pocked by iron and copper mines, with the Keweenaw Peninsula jutting out into Lake Superior like the tassel on a lumberjack's cap.

The Lower Peninsula is low-lying country and generally flat. A few ridges, called "eskers" by geologists and "hogbacks" by farmers, wander across the state. They have been built up of gravel and stones dug out by the glaciers. On both sides of the Lower Peninsula the land slopes downward, to Lake Huron on the east and Lake Michigan on the west. Each has miles and miles of sandy beach.

Lake Michigan in early postglacial times was much larger than it is

Lake Michigan dune country

Grand Sable dunes

today. As the lake decreased to its present size, it left huge sand dunes lining the shores from Indiana to Traverse City. Some of these dunes, covered with brush and trees and appearing to be small rounded hills, are now as much as thirty miles inland. For two hundred miles along the lake shore, they rise fifty to a hundred feet from the beach. Some of these are "dead" dunes. That is, they are covered by vegetation and stay in place, since the plant roots keep the wind from shifting the sand about. But others are open to the winds, which normally blow from the west and northwest. These winds push the sand ahead in a relentless march, filling in the hollows and covering the brush and trees. A few towns and a good deal of farm- and forestland lie buried under them. Sleeping Bear Dune, the largest of them all, soars up six hundred feet from the shore near Frankfort, piled as steeply as sand will lie. Vacationers can ride over it in special cars equipped as "dune buggies." In places they can even ski down the fine sand of its sides.

People who live in Michigan sometimes forget that Michigan is made up of water almost as much as it is of land. Its coastline is more than three thousand miles long. It has within its total area almost as many square miles of lakes as it has of land. There are no big rivers in Michigan, but thousands of smaller streams. The St. Joseph and the Kalamazoo Rivers in southwestern Michigan are the largest, but they are not long. The Grand River meanders through the center of the state toward Lake Michigan, while the swift Muskegon, to the north, flows westward, too. These waterways were very convenient for both the Indians and the early traders. By paddling a canoe to the source of one of the many rivers that flowed east toward Lake Huron, then making a short portage overland to the headwaters of a river flowing west, the traveler could cross the state quite easily at several places. Later these streams helped the pioneers to penetrate quickly into the center of the state and settle the land.

Lying between Lake Michigan and Lake Huron, the Lower Peninsula has a climate neither so cold in winter nor so warm in summer as the climates of its sister Lake states. The vast expanses of water that surround it help control the temperature of the air. Lake Michigan rarely freezes over where the water is deep. It warms the gales that blow across it from the northwest so that they are not so frigid as they

are in Wisconsin and Minnesota. In the summer both Lake Michigan and Lake Huron cool the hot, dry winds from the southwest prairies. This is not true in the Upper Peninsula, where the snows pile up in ten-foot drifts in winter, and where you may wake up on a May morning to find a light frost.

What the early explorers noted first about Michigan were the trees. Of the state's 37,000,000 acres of land, 35,000,000 were once forest — a vast sea of trees, broken only by lakes, streams and small patches of grassland known as "oak openings" or sometimes "prairies." All of Europe has only eight kinds of trees; Michigan has eighty-five, including four kinds of ash, three of maple, five of poplar, and thirteen different kinds of oak.

What trees grow in Michigan, and where, depends on the kinds of soil the glacier left and the amount of moisture in it. In the southern

A Michigan forest

part of the state, below an imaginary line that stretches from Saginaw to Grand Haven, there were and still are the hardwoods — ash, hickory, maple, oak, beech, elm. In swampy or marshy areas, larch, spruce, tamarack, and cedar grow. The great pine forests were once north of this line. They stretched to the tip of the Upper Peninsula — the tall, soaring white pine, the majestic red pine, the smaller jackpine. Lumber companies logged almost all this off in less than a century. Only about eighty acres of the original stand of pine is left in the Lower Peninsula, along with fifteen million acres of land where the trees have long since been cut. Bit by bit this land is being replanted and reclaimed, so that someday Michigan will perhaps look a little more as it did when the explorers came. There are now long stretches of this second-growth timber, miles of it, for the hunter and camper and hiker.

These woods and streams are filled with game and fish, certainly as much or more of them than when only Indians lived in Michigan. Michigan's trout are known the world over, and so are its other game fish. The grayling, once the state's most popular variety, disappeared a half-century ago. The state's most unusual fish, the smelt, is a herringlike fish that in season rushes from the northern parts of Lake Michigan and Lake Huron up the river mouths in such numbers that people dip them up in pails and tubs.

Michigan's forests support great herds of deer — many more than when the Indians hunted them — and a surprisingly large population of black bears. In lean seasons, the bears sometimes wander into small towns to search for food. Wolves, once numerous in pioneer days, are almost gone, except for a few hidden deep in the Upper Peninsula forests. The caribou disappeared with the passenger pigeons, which were once so thick that they broke the branches of the trees they rested on.

Deer

Pheasant

The last great flock of passenger pigeons seen in Michigan, in 1878, was forty miles long and from three to ten miles wide. Now there are none. But pheasants are so numerous that every farmer finds them in his cornfields, and they turn up in suburban householders' backyards. Hunters bag nearly a million pheasant each year.

Nature has been generous to Michigan. It gave the state a fairly mild climate, put it in the center of the Great Lakes — the largest portion of the entire world's supply of fresh water — and gave it trees, minerals, fertile reaches of land, woods and streams for its people to enjoy. Some of what nature gave was wasted, and some of it was simply used up, but many of nature's gifts are permanent. The face of the land is still beautiful, as it was to the pioneers, and its promise, as it was to them, is still unlimited.

Chapter 3

The Day of the Red Man

The first men came to the region that is now Michigan about six thousand years ago. They were Indians, and little is known about them. We know that they built mounds in which they buried their dead, made simple gardens, hunted, fished and mined, but they left few traces by which we can reconstruct how they lived.

Whatever tribes these earlier people belonged to, the Indians who met the first explorers of the region in the seventeenth century were Algonquins. They were part of the great family of Indians who occupied most of Ontario, all of the Great Lakes area, and the northwest lands of Minnesota and the Dakotas. Another great family of North American Indians, the Iroquois, lived in eastern Canada and in what is now New York State. The Five Nations, a warlike alliance of Iroquois tribes, were traditional enemies of the Algonquins; wherever the lands held by the two met, there was constant war.

Indian burial grounds

Michigan Indians

The Algonquins had been in Michigan at least a hundred years when the French came. The most powerful tribes were the Chippewa (also called Ojibwa), who lived in the Upper Peninsula and the eastern half of the Lower Peninsula; the Ottawa, who lived in the western Lower Peninsula; and the Pottawatomi, who occupied most of the southern edge of Michigan. These three tribes, so closely related that they sometimes held intertribal council meetings, called themselves "The Three Fires." A few Miamis lived in the southwestern portion of Michigan, some Mascoutins in the central Grand River Valley, a group of Sauks in the Saginaw Valley ("Saginaw" means "place of the Sauks") and some Menominees at the western end of the Upper Peninsula. Later, when the pressure of white settlement and Iroquois warfare increased, the Sauks left Michigan to join their brothers the Foxes in Illinois. The Mascoutins and Miamis were pushed westward toward the Mississippi. A small group of Hurons or Wyandots, an Iroquoian tribe forced out of Canada by the Five Nations, settled near Detroit and were eventually pushed westward, too.

Michigan's Indian population was never large. Winters were too long and cold to support much agriculture of the primitive kind the Indians knew, and game was not plentiful enough to provide food for many hunters. Historians have estimated that perhaps 15,000 Indians lived in Michigan in the early days, most of them in the Lower Peninsula. Although it is difficult to estimate the numbers in each tribe, there were probably more Chippewas than others, with the Ottawas next and the Pottawattomi tribe third in size.

All of them lived in the Neolithic or Stone Age stage of human cultural development. They lived by hunting and agriculture, made tools of stone, used the bow and arrow and knew little of the uses of metal. None of the Algonquin tribes had so strong an artistic or political tradition as, for example, the Navaho in the Southwest states or the Iroquois in the East. Nor were they so nomadic and warlike as the plains tribes of the West. Michigan Indians lived chiefly by farming, with the hunters supplying meat to go with the staple crops of corn, beans, squash and a few other vegetables. Their agricultural methods were simple and crude. They moved their villages about frequently, following the seasons and the movements of game, working small patches of soil and then moving on to new ones, returning a year or two later.

All of the tribes except the Chippewas lived in dome-shaped lodges covered with bark or matting over frameworks of poles. The Chippewas built the familiar cone-shaped tepees, covering them with bark rather than skins, since trees were more plentiful than animals. More than seven hundred Indian-village sites have been located in Michigan. Remains of their garden patches can still be seen in places undisturbed by the farmer's plow.

The red man and the white man in early Michigan lived together fairly well, except for their inability to understand each other's view of property. Among the Indians, private ownership of land was practically unknown. Hunting and fishing grounds belonged to the whole tribe, and were open equally to anyone in the tribe. A few items were thought of as belonging to a particular person or family — weapons, ornaments, shelter, clothes — but otherwise no Indian thought of actually *owning* something. When the Indians signed treaties to sell land, it was difficult for them to understand exactly what they were selling. When the white man claimed that a particular piece of ground and everything on it belonged to him and him only, the Indian was often puzzled and angry. Nor were these treaties always honored by the white men. The history of agreements between white men and Indians in Michigan, as elsewhere in North America, is too often one of broken pledges. The traders used guns, rum and promises to sweep the Indians from the land and open it to the trappers, the settlers, and the farmers. Of all the means they used, the treaty was the most effective.

Despite this, there were exceptionally few major conflicts between Indians and the French, English and Americans who came to the area, over the two hundred years from its discovery to its admission as a state to the Union. After their early explorations of the Great Lakes in the seventeenth century, the French settled down to develop the fur trade. French traders and trappers did little to disturb the Indian's traditional way of life. Sometimes they married Indian girls, and often found no great reason to change those ways of Indian life that did not ship for much of their trade in furs. The missionaries, who arrived soon after the explorers, hoped to convert the Indians to Christianity. They found no great reason to change those ways of Indian life that did not conflict with the teachings of the church. It was not always easy to adjust the conflicts that were bound to occur between two such different cultures. But for a long time, the two peoples managed to live together in comparative peace.

During the eighteenth century, the situation began to change. As settlers flooded into New York, Pennsylvania, and Ohio, and along the St. Lawrence Valley, the Iroquois pressed against the Algonquin tribes to the west. The French and British took more and more territory from the tribes. Hunting grounds and game supplies decreased. In the later seventeenth century, France and Britain had begun a bitter struggle for the control of North America. This war was known as the Seven Years' War, in American history usually called the French and Indian Wars. All Indian tribes east of the Mississippi River became pawns in this great contest between the European powers. While the Michigan tribes were not so fully engaged as the Iroquois to the east, their fate was equally at stake. The British used as allies the Iroquois; the French, their ancient enemies the Algonquins. When war came in 1756, Indians and Frenchmen from Detroit and Michilimackinac marched east to fight the British. In 1760 the French took down their flag at Detroit for the last time, and in 1763, with the Treaty of Paris, France gave up all its North American empire to British rule.

Without the help of their French allies, the Algonquins of the Great Lakes area were doomed. They did not like the English, who were the allies of the Iroquois. While the English held no particular ill will against them, their rule over the Indians was far more rigorous than that of the French. As English and then American settlers moved into the area, the Indians were forced westward and northward toward the upper portion of the Lower Peninsula and the Upper Pensula, where neither the land nor the forests could sustain them. Sometimes soldiers simply ordered tribes to leave their ancient lands. Other times land companies or individual purchasers bought the land cheaply and moved in. Poverty-stricken and leaderless, the Indian population had few defenses. Some went to Canada, others moved out toward the West, where they faced the fierce and hostile plains tribes. The ones who remained in Michigan tried without much success to adjust to white society. When the United States took possession of the Michigan

35

region after the American Revolution, the Indians gradually gave up their lands to the settlers by a series of treaties.

In 1854, the federal government established reservations for exclusively Indian use. Indians were allowed later to sell their reservation lands, which they did, bit by bit, so that little reservation land remains today. There are, in fact, only four: Isabella, near Mount Pleasant; L'Anse, on Keeweenah Bay in Lake Superior; Bay Mills, northeast of Brimley; and Hannahville, just west of Escanaba. The Indians who live on these reservations total not much more than a thousand. However, the present-day Indian population in Michigan has tended to concentrate around former reservation lands so that several predominantly Indian settlements still exist. There are Ottawas and Chippewas in northwestern lower Michigan near Cross Village and Harbor Springs and in central Michigan. A number of Ottawas and Pottawatomis live in the Upper Peninsula.

What did the Indians leave in Michigan? They left their names, of course, scattered across the map. The French left theirs — Grand

Marais, L'Anse, Cadillac, Detroit — and the British, theirs too — Drummond Island, Lake George, Williamston. But before the names were left by the Frenchman and the Englishman and the American the old Algonquin names were there. The name "Michigan" (meaning "fish-catching place") and Michilimackinac, "island of the big turtle," are both pure Indian. There are dozens more. There are the names of long-gone chiefs, such as the Pottawatomis' Topinabee and Pokagon, the great Ottawa Pontiac, Tecumseh, the Shawnee warrior, and lesser known chiefs like Keewadin and Okemos. There are names that describe places, among them Escanaba ("flat rock"), Muskegon ("marshy place"), Manistique ("red rocks"), Newaygo ("much water"), Kalamazoo ("boiling water pot") and Ishpeming ("high ground"). These are part of the legacy of Michigan.

The Indians also left a network of trails by which French *voyageurs*, English soldiers, and American settlers found their way through the forests. Today, most of their trails lie under Michigan's superhighways. When you drive from Detroit to Chicago, you are really following the old St. Joseph Trail, just as the Sauks and Ottawas once did.

Massacre at Michilimachinac

Michigan Indians

The Grand River Trail went from Detroit to Grand Rapids; the Saginaw Trail wound down from Saginaw Bay to the River Rouge and along the Detroit River. In the Upper Peninsula, the tourist who drives from Wisconsin to St. Ignace and on to Sault Ste. Marie is on the old Green Bay Trail.

Little other physical evidence remains of the once-great tribes who spread across Michigan before the white man came, but the names of the places he lived and the trails he traveled will always bring up memories of the wild and beautiful wilderness that was there when the red man roamed and ruled it.

The most valuable legacy of the Indians is their folklore and legends. The Algonquins had an ancient store of traditional stories, held in common, with slight variations with other Michigan tribes. Many of these tales centered on a half-god, half-devil creature called Manabozho, by some; Manabush or Wenibojo, by others. A fascinating and somewhat puzzling character. Manabozho was not only wise and benevolent, doing many things to help man, but he was also something of a conceited, mischievous, and occasionally cruel trickster. There was also an Iroquois folk hero named Hawawentha or Hiawatha ("wise man"), whose adventures were sometimes mixed in with Manabozho's. When Henry Wadsworth Longfellow wrote his famous "The Song of Hiawatha" in 1854, he selected the best traits of Menabozho and combined them with some of the Hiawatha stories. He created an entirely new character, who was very different from the originals and whose adventures appealed to the popular taste.

In addition to such folk heroes, the Indians had stories about the "manitous" spirits who lived in the lakes and woods. They had control over many of men's affairs. Two were especially important — Gitchi Manito, "The Good One," who taught the Indians how to raise food, build shelter and govern themselves; and Gitchi Manido, "The Evil One," who brought famine, sickness, war and death. These two spirits contended eternally for the mastery of man's destiny. There were also the "animal fathers," Rabbit, Turtle, Owl, Bear, and all the others who lived in the forests before man came and who still retained great power over crops, hunting, weather and daily life.

To the Indians everything in the sky above and the earth below

39

Sleeping Bear dune

held meanings and messages. Their legends provided explanations of how the world was created, of the personalities of animals and the uses of plants, and an insight into the forces of nature. Out of these elements they built a rich, imaginative and complex body of folk literature, handed down orally from generation to generation.

Some of the stories explained how certain places were created or how they were named. Mackinac Island, the story went, was the first island in the world. The Great Spirit made it by heaping earth on the back of the Great Turtle, an animal spirit sacred to the Chippewas. Sleeping Bear Dune is a mother bear who tried to swim across Lake Michigan with her two cubs. When the cubs drowned, Gitchi Manito created the two Manitou Islands offshore to mark their graves, and let the mother bear sleep forever in sight of them.

The Chippewa legend of the creation of the earth is one of the most delicately told of all. After the Flood, the Great Manito was floating over the waters on a raft filled with all the creatures. He wanted some

land brought up to him so that he could build a new place for man and all the animals, birds and plants to live. He asked the beaver, proud king of the water and the most powerful swimmer of all, to dive down into the deep to find land. The beaver dived, stayed for hours, and came up without having touched bottom. Next the quick and skillful otter tried. He stayed down longer, and finally broke the surface exhausted and unsuccessful. Manito was ready to give up, when the humble, lowly muskrat volunteered to try. He dropped awkwardly overboard with a thump and quickly sank. All night Manito and the animals waited, fearing that the muskrat must be dead. But at dawn, as daylight broke, Manito saw the muskrat's body floating in the water and pulled it to the raft. His little paws were shut tightly together, and in one of them Manito found a single grain of sand. The muskrat succeeded where the others failed, though it cost his life. Out of the grain of sand Manito made the earth for man and all the creatures to live in.

Chapter 4

"Seas of Sweet Water"

Of the Great Lakes states, Michigan is the one most closely related to those inland freshwater seas. Michigan touches on all of them except Lake Ontario. Four of them form almost all Michigan's boundaries. They provide transportation, scenery, wealth, resources and recreation for Michigan's people. In large part, the Lakes have determined the course of Michigan's history.

The Jesuits who built missions on their shores called them "Seas of Sweet Water." The first explorers were convinced that they led the way to the Pacific Ocean and the Orient. Since there was nothing like these majestic lakes in all of Europe, the explorers could not fully grasp their extent. Jean Nicolet, who entered the Straits of Mackinac in 1634 with Indian canoemen, carried a wonderfully brocaded Mandarin robe to wear when he met the Great Khan of China, as he fully expected to do. Through the Lakes explorers found their way directly

Lake Michigan

into the core of the continent. Over the Lakes came the traders, soldiers, farmers, miners, lumbermen and all the others who built Michigan, settled the country and made it bloom and produce. No one can think of Michigan without thinking of the Lakes.

The five Lakes are a product of the Glacial Age that shaped the Midwest. At some remote geologic time, they drained westward through Chicago to the Mississippi River and on south to the Gulf of Mexico. But as the glaciers advanced and receded, the flow reversed and poured the melting waters along the St. Lawrence to the Atlantic Ocean. A slight tip of the North American continent — perhaps thirty feet or less — would be enough to send the Lakes rushing down the Chicago-Illinois river system again, draining the St. Lawrence Valley dry and turning the Great Lakes basin into a dreary wasteland, as it was in the Glacial Age.

The Lakes have their own individualities. Lake Superior, which

Lake Superior

Lake Huron

fronts on Michigan's Upper Peninsula, is the largest — a thousand feet deep, blue-black, ice-laden in winter and cold in summer, an imperial inland sea of long distances and arctic storms. Lake Huron, second in size, is chiefly a commercial lake shared with Canada. Its ports are home for tankers, freighters, barges and fishermen. In November, the worst of the storm months, ship captains treat Lake Huron with great respect. Lake Michigan is deep, busy, unpredictable. Car ferries and freighters crisscross it briskly day and night. Vacationers flock to its miles of packed sand beaches. Racing sailboats dot its surface in good weather. Its storms are sudden and lethal. In bad weather on Lake Michigan even the big lakeboats will run for a lee shore. Shallow, choppy Lake Erie, where the Detroit River discharges its shipping, really belongs more to Ohio, though it has provided a gateway to Michigan since the early days. Lake Ontario is more important to New York. On these Lakes, Indians, French, British

45

and Americans have made Michigan's past and shaped its present.

The first sailing vessel to penetrate into the big Lakes was the famous *Griffon,* built in 1679 at the order of the French governor at Quebec, Robert Cavalier, Sieur de la Salle. He dreamed of launching a fleet of ships for the glory and profit of imperial France, one that could carry settlers and traders deep into the wilderness and bring out the bales of furs that put gold in the King's coffers.

La Salle planned to make New France a continental commercial empire, with the Great Lakes at its center. The main trade route, as he saw it, traced down the St. Lawrence Valley to the Lakes, where a Lake fleet would move goods to the French posts in the Illinois country. They in turn would ship the goods down the Mississippi River to the sea and Europe.

The key to La Salle's project was a Lake fleet. In January of 1679 he sent a crew of workmen to establish a boatyard above Niagara Falls. By early summer they had completed a small sailing ship of forty-five tons. La Salle named it the *Griffon,* after a legendary beast supposed to be half lion and half eagle. The *Griffon* was launched in late summer and La Salle, with Father Hennepin, a company of soldiers and a picked crew, set sail on Lake Erie.

The *Griffon* made Detroit in three days of easy sailing. After searching its way up the Detroit River, it sailed into a beautiful lake, covered with flocks of wild geese and swans. La Salle named it Lac Sainte Claire. They stopped to hunt turkeys, catch fish and kill a bear, and thus provisioned set out into Lake Huron. The *Griffon* was now in dangerous waters, unknown to its inexperienced crew. When a huge storm broke out of Thunder Bay, the little ship had its first test. Father Hennepin recorded that all the crew fell on their knees in prayer, except one old saltwater veteran who "did nothing at all except curse and swear against M. La Salle" for sending them to sea in such a cockleshell. One or the other must have worked, for the *Griffon* rode out the storm and in late August dropped anchor at St. Ignace, the French mission and trading post at the Straits of Mackinac. All the soldiers, priests and *voyageurs* welcomed the little craft as it boomed into port with sails set, while the Indians looked on in amazement at the "canoe-that-flies-with-wings."

46

The Griffon

La Salle took on a load of furs at St. Ignace and pushed through the Straits across the upper reaches of Lake Michigan into Green Bay. Here he loaded more furs and ordered his captain to sail directly southeast, across the Lake, to the French post on the St. Joseph River in lower Michigan. La Salle and the rest of the party started overland for St. Joseph, down the west edge of Lake Michigan and across the southern shore.

The *Griffon* with a crew of six set sail on September 18, 1679, across Green Bay. She was never seen again. Where she went down no one knows, though various ancient wrecks have been claimed to be her remains. In 1890, parts of a hull were found at the western end of the Manitoulin Island chain in northern Lake Michigan. They were identified as probably belonging to a seventeenth- or eighteenth-century vessel. That same year a lighthouse keeper on the Manitoulins discovered four skeletons in a cave, two more nearby, a tarnished watch chain, and some seventeenth-century coins. But the Lakes do not give up their secrets easily, and the fate of the *Griffon* and her unlucky crew will probably never be known.

It was almost a hundred years before a ship as large as the *Griffon* sailed the Lakes again, and two centuries before the great fleets that La Salle dreamed of plied their waters. When the British took control of the Lakes after 1763, they began to build sailing vessels at Niagara and Detroit. Successful trips by two small vessels, the *Huron* and the *Niagara*, encouraged the construction of three more. But by the time of the Revolutionary War, only thirteen sailing ships were on the five Lakes.

The first American-built vessel on the Lakes was the *Detroit*, a warship launched on Lake Erie in 1796, only to be wrecked near Erie a year later. At the beginning of the War of 1812, the United States had only a few vessels in operation on the Lakes. The new American Navy was forced to build hastily some small warships out of green lumber. With these Commodore Oliver Perry won his great victory at the Battle of Lake Erie in 1813. The opening of the Erie Canal in 1825 gave a tremendous boost to Lake shipping, for the canal connected the Lakes with the Atlantic Ocean and with Europe. A boat could sail from Chicago to Buffalo, a distance of a thousand miles, transfer its load to the canal boats, and return with a cargo of Eastern-made or imported goods, all in a matter of weeks. By the 1840's almost five hundred sailing vessels worked the Lakes. Thirty years later, at the peak of the Age of Sail, there were eighteen hundred.

Michigan's forests of oak and pine provided exactly the material needed for shipbuilding, the state's first major industry. Dozens of shipyards lined the shore of Lake Huron, from Detroit beyond Saginaw Bay. Here both timber and skilled workmen were available.

The life of the sailor appealed strongly to the farm and city boys of the nineteenth century. In addition to supplying ships for the Lakes trade, Michigan furnished a good many men who sailed them. The work was hard, the hours long, and the Lakes not to be trusted.

The Lakes sailors, like seamen the world over, put together a whole body of superstitions and lore of their own. They refused to begin a voyage on a Friday (an unlucky day for sailors ever since Phoenician times), and they were convinced that certain ships were cursed with bad luck. The schooner *Augusta,* which had a bad reputation from the day of launching, rammed and sank the *Lady Elgin* on Lake Michigan and finally had to be sold to the ocean trade because crews refused to work on her.

A cross-eyed sailor, a woman cook, a black cat, a hatch-cover put on upside down — all these were bad omens. Just whistling on shipboard or changing a ship's name was a sure way of bringing disaster. Some captains placed money under the mainmast for good luck; others believed that tossing a coin over the stern at the start of a voyage insured a good trip.

A few of these beliefs remain today. It is still not a good idea for a sailor to whistle on shipboard until he finds out how his mates feel about it. And the captain of a Mackinac racing sloop may toss a coin overboard, just to make sure.

These white-winged sailors carried most of the goods that the Midwest shipped out to the world — grain from Chicago and Milwaukee for the flour mills of New York, iron ore for the furnaces of Pennsylvania and Ohio, lumber to build the growing cities of the East and West.

Near the end of the century, steamboats finally drove them off the Lakes.

Chapter 5

The Age of Steam

Gradually, as steam replaced sail, the swift white-winged ships dotted the Lakes no more. Robert Fulton's *Clermont* began to ply the Hudson River in 1807. Eleven years later the side-wheeler *Walk-in-the-Water* (as the Indians named it), the first steamboat on the Lakes, puffed awkwardly into Lake Erie. Built of sound white oak, a hundred and thirty-five feet long, the *Walk-in-the-Water* was impressive as she steamed along at six miles an hour, sparks flying and paddle wheels churning. She made the round trip from Buffalo to Detroit and back in two weeks, with stops at Erie, Cleveland, and other ports. She even splashed her way to Mackinac Island and Green Bay now and then. She ran aground in November (always an unlucky month on the Lakes), but her engines and fittings were reclaimed for her successor, the *Superior*.

After that came the *Henry Clay,* the *Pioneer,* and dozens of others.

50

Sketched from Canada shore.
Aug. 1820.
Detroit in the distance.

Walk-in-the-Water

By 1832, the steamers reached Chicago, and by 1839 eight of them were making scheduled runs from Buffalo to Detroit, Chicago and return. The next year the *Vandalia*, the first propeller-driven steamship, appeared on the Lakes and in 1843 the first iron-hulled steamer, the *Michigan*. For years to come, it was still cheaper to haul some kinds of freight by sail, but the new iron steamers took away all the passenger trade and the fast freight. At least two hundred steamships worked the Lakes by the time of the Civil War.

The requirements of Lake commerce led to the development of specially constructed vessels to meet these needs. Recognizing that a great deal of Lake freight consisted of bulk cargoes such as ore, grain, coal and the like, shipbuilders designed a unique freighter. Because these ships were never far from shore, they needed to carry

smaller amounts of fuel and supplies than ocean-going freighters fitted for long voyages. Since most of the hold could be used for cargo, these freighters were designed simply as huge empty hulls, six hundred or more feet long, with the necessary machinery placed at the stern, a pilot house on the bow, and nothing between but a yawning hold that could carry 20,000 tons of coal or ore. Another kind of vessel developed for the Lakes was the ice-breaker, constructed with a thick steel hull capable of easily snapping ice two feet thick.

Like the freighter, the car ferry is a distinctive product of the Great Lakes. Since Lake Michigan lay directly across Michigan's routes to the West, all traffic had to go around it, either to the North or South. In 1866, an enterprising steamship firm built a boat to carry railroad cars across the Detroit River from Canada. Soon afterward someone

Coast Guard icebreaker

thought of doing the same thing across Lake Michigan. Today giant steel car ferries swallow entire trains to transfer them over the Lakes winter and summer, day and night, carrying more rail freight over water than anywhere else in the world.

Jean Nicolet, on his exploring trip westward from Canada in 1634, reported that he passed from Lake Huron into Lake Superior by portaging around a swift and dangerous stretch of rapids that blocked the passage between the two lakes. Two French Jesuit priests who found a tribe of Indians living by these rapids in 1641 called the place "Sault Sainte Marie," or "Falls of the St. Mary's." In time, they founded a mission there. A settlement grew, and after the territory became part of the United States, the "Soo," as people called it, became an important transfer point for trade on the upper Lakes.

The earliest traders recognized the need for a way of bypassing the Falls, which prevented even the smallest boats from going between Lake Superior and Lake Huron. All boats had to be portaged from one lake to the other and all cargoes laboriously hauled through the woods to loading docks. The French dug a small canal around part of the rapids, and American traders built a tramway, which made the transfer of freight somewhat easier. However, the Sault Ste. Marie simply blocked all important commerce between Lake Superior and the other Lakes, in a sense cutting off northern Michigan, Wisconsin, and Minnesota from the rest of the country.

The discovery of rich copper and iron deposits in the Upper Peninsula during the 1840's made it necessary to find some way to go around the Falls. Michigan had been made a state in 1837. Its government asked Congress for assistance in building a canal, but it took time to make a case. It was difficult for Eastern and Southern Congressmen to understand why a canal was needed in the wilderness, where only Indians lived. Senator Henry Clay said it was obviously unnecessary to build anything in "a place quite beyond the remotest settlement in the United States, if not in the moon," which is apparently how Michigan looked to a Kentuckian at the time. Finally, in 1851, Congress granted Michigan 750,000 acres of land from the public domain, the sale of which would finance the construction of a canal at Sault Ste. Marie.

Charles Harvey at Sault Ste. Marie

The Soo locks

The idea appealed to the imagination of a young Vermonter, Charles T. Harvey, who had visited Michigan's Upper Peninsula and was struck by its beauty and potential. Harvey interested a number of influential Eastern businessmen in the proposal, formed a company to bid on the job, and successfully petitioned the Michigan legislature for the contract. The company appointed Harvey general supervisor and in late 1852 he began to buy tools, equipment and supplies. The next spring he shipped them all to Sault Ste. Marie, with four hundred workmen and a hundred mules.

Even Harvey, who had planned it with the utmost care, did not fully realize the enormity of the project. There were no railroads to the Sault Ste. Marie, and everything had to be shipped hundreds of miles up Lake Huron. Since winter closed the lake route, everything had to be ordered and shipped ahead of time. The labor force the next year numbered two thousand men, and Harvey had to build a complete town, including a hospital, from the ground up. In winter, the

A freighter goes through the Soo Canal

temperature plummeted to forty below zero. An epidemic of typhoid and cholera swept through the shanties; hands and feet and faces froze; mules dropped dead; equipment broke or wore out. At one point, the Indians threatened to attack the camp if Harvey's crew disturbed their traditional burying grounds. But young Harvey drove the work relentlessly forward, and almost exactly two years from the starting date, he opened the gate that let the waters of Lake Superior flow into two locks, each three hundred and fifty feet long and seventy feet wide, which would raise and lower ships from one level to the other. On June 18, 1855, the side-wheeler *Illinois*, flags flying and whistle blowing, made the first passage, marking the completion of one of the most spectacular engineering feats of the era.

The Soo Canal at Sault Ste. Marie opened up the whole north country, and made Michigan truly a maritime state. Railroads quickly reached up into the north country, and copper ore, iron ore and lumber began to pour out of upper Michigan to Detroit and on to the East and

West. Harvey's two locks were soon overworked. Another lock opened in 1881, another in 1896, and three more in recent years. Today a ship can pass through every sixteen minutes. The Soo Locks in one day have carried the equivalent of nearly four hundred freight trains forty cars long. All day and all night the long Lake ships slide through the Canal, their hoarse hoots resounding across the river where Nicolet's Hurons once paddled their canoes, and where *voyageurs* once portaged on their way to Montreal.

The passenger on a Lake steamer or the traveler looking down on the Lakes from a plane finds it hard to imagine danger in the quiet blue depths. Yet those who follow the Lakes know better. Ever since the *Griffon* sailed off into that Lake Michigan squall long ago, the Lakes have claimed their toll of ships and sailormen. The storms that sweep across them with unrestrained fury now and then serve as a reminder that the Big Sea Water, as the Indians called the Lakes, never will be tamed.

Lake storms strike suddenly and sometimes pass on so quickly that no one is quite sure what has happened. In the 1840's, for example, the steamer *Telegraph* passed Beaver Island on a peaceful day and never appeared again. The passenger steamer *Chicago* left St. Joseph, Michigan, for the short run to Chicago and never arrived. The *Alpena*, seen only thirty-seven miles out of Chicago, never made port. The *Bannock-burn*, a big new steel freighter, rounded Keewenaw Point one winter's day, out of Duluth, and simply disappeared. Eighteen months later an oar marked *Bannockburn* drifted up on the Canadian shore, but no other trace of ship or crew was ever found. These ships, and others like them, no doubt went down in the typically swift and violent winds that sweep across the lakes.

The Indian legends of big winds, and the tales handed down by the French, testify to the stormy history of the Lakes. Modern records naturally are more detailed, but nobody on the Lakes needs to go to the records to recall the disasters of times past. The storm of 1842 took fifty ships and a hundred lives. The big blow of 1869 counted ninety-seven ships and fifty dead. Nor have modern ships been exempt. The great November storm of 1940 tossed six-hundred-foot freighters about like chips, drove six ships ashore, and claimed sixty lives. Even as late as 1958, despite modern shipbuilding methods and meteorological warning systems, the *Carl D. Bradley*, only thirty hours from her home port of Rogers City on the northern shore of the Lower Peninsula, broke up in a Lake Huron storm and went down with all hands. But nothing in the history of the Lakes has yet matched the storm of 1913.

On Saturday, November 8, 1913, the weather bureau at Cleveland predicted snow, wind and unsettled weather for most of the Great Lakes. There was nothing unusual about the report, which was about what Lake captains expected in the blustery winter months. Later in the day, a storm rode into Lake Superior on high winds from the Canadian plains. By Sunday, it seemed to be blowing itself out. But it did not. The winds picked up, barometers began to drop and red storm flags broke out all over the Lakes. Ships scurried for cover, but much too late.

The storm struck with devastating fury. The winds rose to eighty miles an hour and even higher in gusts, swinging wildly from quarter to quarter. One ship in Lake Huron reported a seventy-mile gale from one direction and fifteen-foot waves running in another. The winds continued at hurricane force for sixteen straight hours, lashing every mile of the Lake coasts, throwing up waves thirty feet high and smashing at Lake Huron and Lake Erie with bitter blasts of snow.

When the storm finally rolled eastward, after three long days, it had taken the greatest toll of ships and men ever recorded on the Lakes. The total for all the Lakes was forty ships gone, and two hundred and thirty-five men. The big storm of 1913 still remains fresh in the memory of those who sail the Lakes as testimony to the power of the Wind Spirit who, the Indians believed, lived in the northwest and ruled the waters.

The opening of the St. Lawrence Seaway in 1959 added another dimension to Michigan's relation to the Great Lakes. Built jointly with Canada, the seaway and its seven great locks now bring ships from the seven seas to Michigan's doorstep. Lake craft today sound their traditional salute of welcome — three long and two short whistle blasts — to ocean vessels bearing strange names from Europe and the Orient as they steam from salt to fresh water and on into Michigan

Sailing on the Great Lakes

ports. They unload forty million tons of cargo each year now, and more will come as the locks and channels of the seaway are enlarged and deepened. The furs of John Jacob Astor's American Fur Company went from forest to market by way of sleds, canoes, flatboats, lake sailers, canal boats and steamers. If the American Fur Company were in business now, it could ship beaver skins to Europe by one uninterrupted passage. Michigan could trade today directly with the Great Khan, as Nicolet hoped to do so long ago. The idea of opening the Lakes to the Atlantic Ocean, which began with the first traders who set up their posts at St. Ignace, is now reality. With the St. Lawrence Seaway, Michigan has become part of America's fourth seacoast.

The story of Michigan and the Great Lakes, which opened with a Frenchman searching in the cold northern waters for the passage to China, is still in its early chapters. The animals whose furs meant gold, the Indians who hunted them, and the French and English who traded for them, have gone long ago. The slow lumber barges, the white-sailed packets, the smoking side-wheelers and the awkward whalebacks have long departed, and so have the men who sailed them. But they all were knitted into Michigan's past and became a part of its future. The explorers never found the Great Khan, but the millions who followed them found something more valuable and permanent than the treasures of the Orient — a coronet of lakes, a natural setting for a good life.

Chapter 6

Fur and Pine and Ore

The theme that binds American history together from the sixteenth to the twentieth century is the conquest of the continent. The men from Europe who touched shore with Columbus in the Caribbean, the explorers of New France and of New England, the pioneers who pushed westward through the eastern forests, the settlers who crossed the western plains — all saw a new, shining land that offered unimaginable opportunities and rewards. This westward movement has occupied the energies and dreams of millions of men and women for four hundred years, and Michigan has been very much a part of it.

First came the explorers, then the traders and settlers, then the discovery and use of what the land had to offer. The canoe paddle of the *voyageur*, the axe of the lumberman, the pick of the miner, the scythe of the farmer and the slide-rule of the engineer have each added a brush stroke to the unfinished picture of Michigan. People surged

Forest country

Trading furs

into the region in successive waves, each time drawn by some new way of using the land, each time looking for something — fortune, opportunity, adventure, security, perhaps merely elbow room, or any of a hundred other things. To grasp what Michigan means today, we must look at the history of what the people who came here found in that search.

Furs were found first. The quest for furs drew men into the Michigan wilderness as gold later drew them westward. Europe and the Orient wanted fur for hats, caps, gloves, capes, cloaks and many other articles of clothing. Beaver was the most desirable, since beaver hair made the best grade of felt. But the trade also included fox, mink, otter, marten, lynx, weasel and, to a lesser extent, bear and buffalo. The nobility rated furs along with jewels and gold as valuable possessions. Every poor man dreamed of owning a fur cape or a good beaver hat. North America's furbearing animals made up its greatest source of wealth in the seventeenth century. The search for them influenced the course of exploration, settlement, trade, diplomacy, war and peace over the first century of Michigan's existence.

The French organized the trade carefully and efficiently. The fur companies, who had headquarters at Montreal and Quebec, placed agents at strategic points through the Great Lakes area. The Governor General of New France granted licenses to merchants, who in turn employed *coureurs de bois*, or "rangers of the forest," to trade with the Indians for furs. The *voyageurs*, as these traders were sometimes called, bought the furs, packed them in boats and transported them to the agency posts for shipment to Canada. In a relatively short time, the *voyageurs* developed well-defined routes which penetrated ever deeper into Indian country. Traces of these routes remain today in Minnesota and Ontario. The chief Michigan posts, which were the most important on the Lakes, were at Michilimackinac (St. Ignace), Sault Ste. Marie, and St. Joseph in southern Michigan.

The *voyageurs* furnished a colorful interlude in early Michigan history. Many of them held trading licenses, but a good many probably did not, preferring to sell illegally to English and Dutch agents. They bought trade goods from the post merchants — blankets, beads, guns, powder, pots, hatchets, knives and the like — and exchanged them with the Indians for marketable furs. To them the wilderness was home, much as it was to the Indians. Their trips took months, even years, and some of them married into the tribes and adopted Indian customs.

The fur trade in the region reached its highest point of organization by 1660. Although France gave way to England, and England to the United States, fur trading remained more or less the same for the next hundred and fifty years. The English Hudson's Bay Company and Astor's American Fur Company continued to operate in the same way.

While it lasted, the trade in furs that poured out of Michigan and the Great Lakes country brought tremendous fortunes to the fur companies. It was not unusual for a merchant to make a profit of a thousand percent on the trade goods he sold to be exchanged for furs, and for the company to make another thousand percent profit when it marketed its bales in Europe. A keg of gunpowder, for example, which cost two dollars in London, could be traded for beaver skins which, when sold in the London market, were worth one hundred and forty dollars. For almost two hundred years the fur companies drained wealth out of the Michigan woods. In 1789, for example, one company alone shipped out 185,000 skins, more than 100,000 of them beaver.

Eventually it had to end. The supply of furbearing animals could not last. The game grounds were gradually hunted out, and settlers cut down more and more of the forest, where beaver and foxes lived, to plant their farms. Furs lost their value as fashions changed and as methods of textile manufacture improved. When John Jacob Astor retired from the fur business in 1834 (the richest man in American history up to his time) the trade was rapidly declining, except in the Far West.

Though the fur trade brought wealth to the fur companies and the merchants, it destroyed the red man's culture. The Indian became dependent on hunting for his living. As soon as he adopted the white man's goods, he had to give up all his other activities to concentrate on searching for furs to buy goods. When the supply of animals began to decrease, Indian hunters had to go farther afield to find them, bringing on a series of bloody wars between tribes over hunting rights.

Within fifty years after the arrival of the trader, the tribes depended on him for knives, blankets, guns, traps and dozens of other manufactured items, including needles, which only furs could buy. "The gift of iron," as one Pottawatomi chief called it, that the white man brought to the Indian, also spelled his doom. Brandy and rum, both introduced by the traders, had even more devastating effects on Indian life.

Lumber came after furs. Cut from the great green sea of hardwood and pine that covered ninety percent of Michigan, it became the main source of wealth. To build settlements in frontier country required boards. While Michigan was still under British rule, a few sawmills existed along the St. Clair River. As the demand for building materials

Sawmill

increased, lumbermen moved into the heavily forested Saginaw Val-
.ley, where the lumbering industry really got its start in the 1830's.
The Saginaw forests of white pine, towering a hundred and fifty feet
skyward, were easily reached by small rivers that laced through them.
Soon the axemen spread out over all of northeastern Michigan. There
were so many trees, the lumbermen believed, that the supply would
last for centuries.

After the Civil War the demand for lumber was so great that Michigan's great virgin forests could hardly satisfy it fast enough. A growing
nation needed houses, stores, factories, buildings of every kind, and
needed them immediately. (Michigan lumber, for example, rebuilt
nearly all of Chicago after its great fire of 1871.) Since the forests of

Lumberjacks

The Day Spring, *a lumber schooner*

the Eastern states were almost gone, lumbermen by the thousands rushed into Michigan. Timberland was cheap and easy to obtain. Forests belonging to the federal and state governments were often sold for what they would bring or for a minimum set price. Lumber companies bought acre upon acre of Michigan white pine, the finest in the world, for prices as low as $1.25 an acre, stripped it, and moved on. "Here today and gone tomorrow," wrote a contemporary observer of the scene, "was the watchword of the times. Get rich and get out."

Saginaw, the logging capital of Michigan in the early days of the boom, stood at the center of eight hundred lumber camps. It employed 25,000 lumberjacks who, when they chose to spend their paychecks in town, made Saginaw rock. The smell of sawdust from Saginaw drifted far out over Lake Huron. Ship captains could find their way into the bay in a fog by following their noses. Bay City, Alpena, Sheboygan, and other lumber towns along the Lake Huron shore were smaller Saginaws. When the loggers moved westward, the Lake Michigan ports — South Haven, Manistee, Pentwater, Ludington, Muskegon — followed the same pattern, and when they moved north, so did Upper Peninsula towns like Seney, Germfask, Newberry, Dollarville and others. Money came and went fast in the logging towns. Those who could hang on to it made fortunes.

Lumberjacks were hard, tough men who worked long hours for small pay. Men of every nationality came from many countries to follow the camps through Michigan — French-Canadians from the Eastern forests, Swedes, Finns, Germans, Poles, Irish, Danes and many others.

When the lumber companies moved into a forest, they sent in first a group of men called "timber cruisers" who marked the trees to be cut. Sawyers cut the trees down, axemen trimmed off the branches, and "buckers" sawed the logs into lengths of twelve to twenty feet. "Swampers," driving teams of horses or oxen, hauled the logs to a river or narrow-gauge railroad for transportation to the mills. If the logs were to be floated downstream, lumberjacks called "river hogs" gathered them into raftlike masses and guided them on their way. Though it was swift, the process of logging off a stand of timber was seriously inefficient. Historians have estimated that for every tree turned into lumber, nine others were wasted. The bottoms of many Michigan rivers and lakes today are lined with logs left from the old timber drives.

The lumber men who thought the trees would last forever were dead wrong. The great timber boom was soon over, surprisingly fast. In 1870 Michigan was first among the states in lumber production, with one hundred and five sawmills at work in the Saginaw Valley alone. The peak year was 1888, when the state produced five billion board-feet of lumber from two thousand sawmills. But faster than anyone had ever thought possible, the forests disappeared. Millions of acres of stumps, brush, tangled branches, fire-scarred land, and dozens of dying lumber towns were left behind. In 1910 one of the oldtimers, looking around at his home town of Muskegon, wrote, "The finest white pine and hardwood forest in the world is now a desert of fire-blasted stumps and slashings, with rotting piles and moss-covered wharves where once echoed the busy refrain of forty-seven giant sawmills." It was all too true, and although Muskegon came back, many of the once-busy and wealthy lumber towns never did. In Sheboygan there still exists, as a kind of memorial to the great old days, what the residents call "Sawdust Mountain," a pile of sawdust a thousand feet long and a hundred feet high. This is about all that is left of the majestic blanket of pine trees that once spread over Michigan.

A Michigan forest

Copper and iron were Michigan's next discovery. Before the trees were gone, men found the great mineral wealth stored in the rock underneath Michigan's Upper Peninsula, left there by the volcanoes and glaciers of millions of years ago. The explorers knew from Indian tales that there was copper in Upper Michigan, but since they were chiefly interested in furs the French made no attempt to find it. In 1771, Alexander Henry, the Englishman who found the Ontonagon Boulder, opened a small mine nearby and abandoned it when he failed to find the main lode.

Indians, however, had mined Upper Peninsula copper on the Keweenaw Peninsula and Isle Royale for centuries before the French came. They broke off pieces of copper-bearing rock they found on the surface, heated it, poured cold water on it, and picked the copper out of the veins in the cracked rock. In northern Michigan, thousands of stone hammers and acres of ancient mining pits have been found which date back as far as four thousand years. Articles made of Michigan

Douglass Houghton finds copper

copper have been found in the remains of Indian villages all over the Western hemisphere. Whoever these primitive miners were, their trade reached far beyond Michigan. By the time the French came, the tribes had for some reason lost much of the art of extracting and working copper and the old mines had long been filled with vegetation and rubble.

The man who discovered what the Indians had almost forgotten and what the French and English cared little about was Douglass Houghton. He was a young Detroit physician who was appointed State Geologist of Michigan in 1837, the year it became a state. Houghton set out to make an inventory of the state's mineral resources. Working through the Upper Peninsula in 1841 Houghton, with his trained scientist's eye, saw geological evidences of huge deposits of both copper and iron. His reports started a copper rush that attracted men from every corner of the country.

Miners, prospectors, and promoters streamed into the Keweenaw and Ontonagon country from every ship that arrived at the Straits of Mackinac or the Sault Ste. Marie. The bulk of the rush centered about Copper Harbor, Hancock, Eagle Harbor, Houghton, and Ontonagon. The federal government even built Fort Wilkins to protect the new towns from the Indians who, as it turned out, were much less troublesome than miners in town on a Saturday night.

The Cornishmen came first. They were professional miners. Cornishmen had worked the mines in England since Roman days. They taught the trade to the French-Canadians, Scandinavians, Finns, Poles and Italians who came to the Upper Peninsula on the heels of the rumors, and left their imprint permanently there. Upper Peninsula towns exist today in which ninety percent of the people are of Cornish descent, and the Cornish miner's pasty — a meat pie baked in dough, to be carried in the pocket and reheated with a miner's candle on the blade of a shovel — is one of Michigan's most delectable treats. The Finns, both foresters and miners, still are one of the largest national groups in the Upper Peninsula, where villages such as Toivola, Nisula, Tapiola, Kiva, and Rock are almost wholly Finnish settlements.

By the late 1840's dozens of mining companies were hard at work in the copper country. Some struck it rich, most did not. The Cliff

Mine found a huge deposit in 1844 and eventually took forty million pounds of pure copper out of the ground. Samuel Knapp, prospecting near the present town of Rockland in 1848, found some old Indian mining pits. He dug down and uncovered a chunk of nearly pure copper ten feet long, weighing four tons. Underneath it was the beginning of a vein that made his Minnesota Mine the richest ever discovered in Michigan. In 1856, another company opened the Calumet Lode, which was worked for seventy years before the mine closed. One shaft of the Calumet-Hecla mine goes down for nearly two miles.

The story of iron was much the same. William Burt, a surveyor working with a party near Negaunee in the Upper Peninsula in 1844, found his compass needle swinging about so wildly as to be useless. Searching about, Burt discovered red outcroppings of magnetic iron ore. He had found what was to become the great Marquette Iron Range. Philo Everett and some companions heard of Houghton's and Burt's surveys and came north to investigate. Local Indians told them of "heavy stones" that possessed magic properties and led them to the forests near Teal Lake. Among the roots of a fallen pine Everett picked

Steel Mill

out handfuls of these "heavy stones." Not far away he found a long exposed ridge of rich iron ore. The Jackson Mining Company, formed on the basis of his discovery, was one of the richest, but it was only one of a hundred and twenty mining corporations working in the area by 1850. A few years later miners opened up the Menominee Range, and after that the Gogebic Range. Soon the Upper Peninsula was scattered with mining towns like Vulcan, Iron Mountain, Iron River, and Ironwood.

The mining boom did not last long. By 1879, Michigan was producing more copper than any other area in the world. But when the mass deposits of pure copper began to run out, production costs went up and Michigan found it hard to compete with new mines recently discovered in Montana, Utah and Arizona. When the Mesabi Iron Range opened in Minnesota in 1892 and the supply of high-grade Michigan ore decreased, the center of iron operations moved westward. Though methods have been developed that will make the processing of low-grade taconite ore profitable, it is unlikely that Michigan's mines will ever again be able to compete with those of the rest of the world.

Unloading iron ore

Chapter 7

Putting the Nation on Wheels

By 1900, less than three hundred years after the explorers came, the rich heritage of Michigan's natural resources had almost been exhausted. The trees were nearly gone, the mines used up, millions of acres of land cut over or burned over, eroded, or flooded.

There had always been farming, since the days when the French had tilled their ribbon-shaped strips of land at Detroit. Michigan had its share of good land, but there was not enough to go around, or enough to support an expanding twentieth-century economy. At the southern edge of the pine forests in the Lower Peninsula, the soil was good enough to match that of Ohio and Indiana. In the northern half of the state, including the Upper Peninsula, farmers found it hard going on the thin soil of the cut-over lands. With timber and copper and iron going or gone, Michigan at the turn of the century seemed to float along in a backeddy of the stream of national growth.

Detroit

Ransom E. Olds

OLDSMOBILE CURVED DASH RUNABOUT
BUILT FROM 1900 THROUGH 1904

SPECIFICATIONS

CAPACITY -- Two passengers.
WHEEL BASE -- 66 inches.
TREAD -- 55 inches.
FRAME -- Angle steel.
SPRINGS -- Oldsmobile side springs.
WHEELS -- 28-inch wood artillery.
TIRES -- 3-inch detachable.
MOTOR -- 5 x 6-inch 7 H. P. horizontal.
TRANSMISSION -- All-spur gear, two speeds
  forward and reverse.
FINISH -- Black with red trimming.

EQUIPMENT -- Complete set of tools and
  pair of large brass side lamps.
RADIATOR -- Copper disk.
CARBURETOR -- Oldsmobile.
IGNITION -- Jump spark.
STEERING GEAR -- Tiller.
DIFFERENTIAL -- Bevel-gear type.
BRAKES -- Differential and rear wheel.
WATER CAPACITY -- Five gallons.
CIRCULATION -- Gear pump.
GASOLINE CAPACITY -- Five gallons.

Then came the automobile. Here was another chance. This was opportunity, and its name was Detroit, dozing comfortably in the 1890's.

Most people think that the automobile was invented in Detroit. Actually it was not. There had been successful experiments with self-propelled vehicles during the 1880's in both Europe and America. In 1893, at least two different mechanics produced what might be called the first American automobiles, Elwood Haynes in Indiana and the Duryea brothers in Massachusetts. Some months later, in early 1894, two young Detroit mechanics, Charles King and Henry Ford, put together a gasoline engine and a buggylike frame and made an automobile. A year after that another mechanically minded young man, Ransom E. Olds, built an auto in Lansing.

It was Olds who really first put the automobile into production. He believed that the future of the "horseless carriage" lay with the gasoline engine. By 1895, he had built a four-wheeled gasoline carriage that worked fairly well. He tested it on the Lansing streets, found its weak points, and after two years of work on weekends and during evenings, completed another in 1897. This automobile (still on exhibition at the Smithsonian Institution in Washington) was the car he wanted. He formed a company to manufacture and market it, and by 1900, after he had moved his small factory to Detroit, his Olds Motor Works was one of the better-known companies. Olds was constantly experimenting, redesigning and improving. His car was known as a dependable piece of engineering.

At that time the Olds cars were relatively high-priced automobiles designed for a limited market. But in 1900 the Olds company lost money. The directors then decided to build, in addition to their high-priced car, a medium-priced and a low-priced model. While they believed that the real profit lay in expensive, custom-built cars, they were willing to experiment. In 1901, however, a fire broke out in the Olds factory and all that was saved was the model of the proposed low-priced car. This was probably the most fortunate accident in the history of the industry, although it would have been difficult to convince Ransom Olds of it at the time.

What the Olds engineers had built was the famous "curved-dash runabout," a one-cylinder, lever-steered light car that weighed seven hundred pounds and sold for $650.

The Olds runabout proved its worth in a spectacular seven-and-a-half-day drive from Detroit to New York where the mud-spattered, jaunty little car was the talk of the auto show. The huge, glittering nine-passenger cars went almost unnoticed. Here was a cheap, dependable auto within the range of the average man's pocketbook, a car that took the auto off paved city streets and quiet country lanes and put it on the road, any road.

For the first time in the history of the industry, a dealer took a thousand orders for an automobile. Olds sold four thousand of his cars in 1903, five thousand in 1904, and more each year after that. He sold out his interest in the company and made another automobile (the Reo) that also became well known.

With his Model-T, Henry Ford picked up where Olds left off. The Model-T was perhaps the most useful mechanical means of transportation ever invented by man. It took over the mass market that the runabout had first discovered.

Charles King, Ford's mechanic friend from early days, had lost in-

Henry Ford I in a Model-T

terest in automobiles but Henry Ford had not. Working from the model he and King had built, he had made another. In 1896, he was ready to test it on a trial run. Since he needed clear streets, he waited until two o'clock in the morning. It was raining, and his wife held an umbrella over the motor until Ford cranked it up and sputtered off over the wood-block streets, a kerosene lantern hanging from a hook at the front.

Ford's car worked better than he had hoped. He immediately began work on a second, improved model. Within a few months he was bold enough to drive his car in daylight, frightening horses and pedestrians, cursed by teamsters and threatened by irate horse-car conductors. Complaints about his automobile led the city council to pass regulations restricting the right of automobilists to use the streets. Ford was finally forced to appeal to the mayor for help. He received a special permit which allowed him to drive during the day under certain conditions, becoming thereby the first licensed driver in America. His automobiles improved as he worked and worked on them. Thomas

Henry Ford I looks at his Model-T

The assembly line

Edison, the famous inventor (who later became one of Ford's closest friends) inspected Ford's third model and told the newspapers, "The horse is doomed." Even Edison did not realize how right he was.

By then, it seemed that everybody in Michigan was building autos. When Ford quit his job and joined the Detroit Automobile Company in 1899, twenty-five auto firms were in operation. Within ten years a hundred different kinds of cars were being manufactured in Michigan. Competition was keen and the casualties heavy. Who remembers the Cartocar, the Rebacne, the Earl, the Jackson, or the Saxon?

After hundreds of companies formed and failed over the years, the so-called "Big Three," all based in Detroit, came to dominate the industry and do so to this day.

Henry Ford tried twice before he finally founded his own successful company in 1903. He was convinced that an automobile could be manufactured for a mass market, rather than as a rich man's luxury, and he had worked out a simple, efficient and sturdy model that could be produced at a minimum price. The famous Model-T, the car that changed the transportation habits of the world, sold at first for $950 and eventually for as little as $360. To compete with Ford and his cheap, simple machine, every company had to meet the challenge of mass production, with the result that ownership of a car was soon a part of every American's life.

Henry Ford first introduced the concept of the minimum wage into the industry. In January, 1914, he announced that the Ford Motor Company would pay no less than five dollars for an eight-hour shift at its Highland Park plant. Workmen immediately descended on Detroit in such numbers that firemen and police had to be called to break up the mob that stormed the company offices. The result of the announcement reduced labor turnover and increased production, as well as the sales of Fords.

The giant of them all, General Motors, owed its origins to an eccentric business genius, William C. Durant, a carriage-maker from Flint. Between 1908 and 1910, Durant put together all the companies he could buy into one big company. Durant soon challenged Ford for leadership in the industry. General Motors owned four major companies — Buick, Cadillac, Olds, and Oakland — but Durant's daring

William C. Durant   *Walter Chrysler*

business methods got him into trouble. Finding himself gradually pushed out of the company he created, Durant left to organize Chevrolet, which shortly swallowed up General Motors itself, leaving Durant in control of an even larger company than the one he had lost. Unfortunately for him, he lost it again in 1920, along with his personal fortune of $90,000,000. Nevertheless General Motors, one of the largest and wealthiest corporations in the history of modern business, owed its beginnings to Durant's business skill.

The third member of the "Big Three" was built by Walter Chrysler, a former General Motors engineer who put together two fading companies to create the Chrysler Corporation in 1925. These three automobile companies, whose names are synonymous with Detroit, manufacture more than ninety-five percent of all automotive products in the United States and what they do dominates Michigan's economic life.

No one can be quite sure why automobile manufacturing grew in Michigan, instead of someplace else, and grew so swiftly. There were probably a number of reasons that combined to make Michigan the center of this new industry. Detroit had already developed a carriage and bicycle industry. The city served as a center for shipbuilding and marine engines. When Ford and the others came along, Detroit already had a large supply of mechanics and workmen with all the skills needed to place an engine in a four-wheeled carriage. Detroit was also a shipping and rail center within easy range of steel, coal, and lumber. It had something more than these advantages, too. It possessed a concentration of imaginative, able men who were willing to take chances and strike out in new directions.

Some of them, like Ford and Olds, were expert and inventive mechanics. Others, like Henry Leland (who built Cadillac), the Dodge brothers, Walter Chrysler, and W. C. Durant were shrewd, skilled

1902 Cadillac

engineers and businessmen. C. F. Kettering, an ispired rule-of-thumb inventor, devised the self-starter and a dozen other innovations. Frank Canfield, an ex-lumberman, invented the modern sparkplug. David Buick perfected a two-cylinder engine; Louis Chevrolet, a racing driver, pioneered four- and six-cylinder engines. These men, and many others like them, made Detroit live up to its name of "The Motor City." True, Detroit did not invent automobiles, but it did invent the idea that automobiles could be mass-produced by the millions for a mass market of millions. The production men and the entrepreneurs of Detroit worked together to put the world on wheels, and the world has never been the same since.

From a staid, prosperous town, content to make carriages and stoves and bicycles, Detroit suddenly became, within a few decades, a pounding, sprawling city. The factories came, spreading over the farmlands

and pushing into the outskirts with acres of plain, functional buildings that spouted smoke, spewed out endless strings of flatcars and shook the ground day and night with the clank of stamp presses and the staccato hammer of riveters.

People came to Detroit by the thousands, the sons of lumberjacks and miners from the declining north country, farm boys from Tennessee and Kentucky, Negroes from Georgia and Alabama, young immigrants from Poland, Ireland, the Ukraine, Hungary, Greece, Italy, and everywhere else the word about Detroit had reached. Detroit put these two elements together — factories and people — and made out of them a precisely planned chaos called an assembly line. It produced that incredibly intricate mechanism called an automobile out of a hundred different materials and a thousand different pieces. This has been Michigan's greatest achievement in the modern world.

Detroit

Chapter 8

Michigan Is People

. . . from everywhere, of every race, creed, and nationality . . . people who came to find the kind of life they wanted and, having found it, stayed.

The French controlled Michigan for more than a hundred years after the explorers first came. But the number of Frenchmen who actually settled down to stay was surprisingly small. For the most part, they were fur traders and merchants. The *voyageurs* often took Indian wives and disappeared into the tribes. The traders, once having made their profit, usually returned to Montreal, Quebec or France.

The British, who held Michigan for only a few years, were mainly interested in the fur trade. They paid little attention either to attracting settlers or to developing other kinds of commerce and agriculture. Even after the American Revolution, when the wave of pioneer settlement rushed westward, only a trickle reached Michigan.

Harvesting wheat in Saginaw county

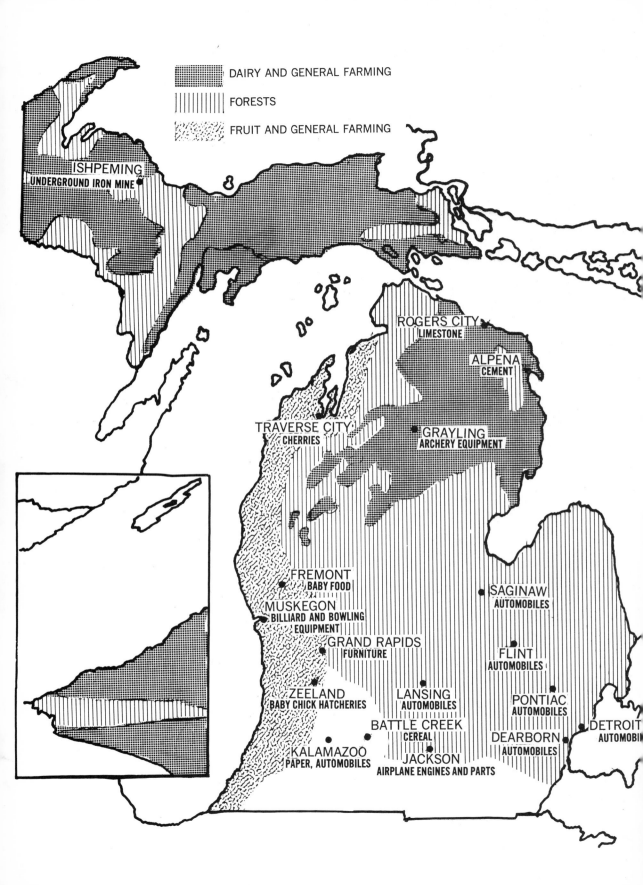

DAIRY AND GENERAL FARMING

FORESTS

FRUIT AND GENERAL FARMING

ISHPEMING
UNDERGROUND IRON MINE

ROGERS CITY
LIMESTONE

ALPENA
CEMENT

TRAVERSE CITY
CHERRIES

GRAYLING
ARCHERY EQUIPMENT

FREMONT
BABY FOOD

SAGINAW
AUTOMOBILES

MUSKEGON
BILLIARD AND BOWLING
EQUIPMENT

GRAND RAPIDS
FURNITURE

FLINT
AUTOMOBILES

ZEELAND
BABY CHICK HATCHERIES

LANSING
AUTOMOBILES

PONTIAC
AUTOMOBILES

BATTLE CREEK
CEREAL

DEARBORN
AUTOMOBILES

DETROIT
AUTOMOBI

KALAMAZOO
PAPER, AUTOMOBILES

JACKSON
AIRPLANE ENGINES AND PARTS

Michigan did not attract settlers in large numbers until its government was established permanently as American. For a long time, rumors had spread in the East that Michigan land was too swampy for good farming. These rumors had been started by the traders, who probably were trying to protect the fur market.

But the farmers who did arrive in Michigan found good dark soil and magnificent forests. They soon sent word back East. First to respond to the reports of good land and clear water in the Michigan country were Americans from New York and New England. By the time Michigan became a state in 1837, they made up two-thirds of the state's population.

By land and by lake, settlers poured into Michigan. The maiden voyage of the *Walk-in-the-Water* from Buffalo, New York, to Detroit in 1818 had opened the way for other passenger steamers. Better roads had been built across northern Ohio to Michigan, which made Eastern markets easier to reach. In 1825, the Erie Canal opened, connecting Michigan and the Great Lakes with New York, New England and the Atlantic ports.

In 1825, the steamers *Pioneer*, *Henry*, and *Superior* landed three hundred passengers a week in Detroit. A decade later, in the summer of 1836, a Detroit newspaperman estimated that a settler's wagon left Detroit every five minutes from sunup to sundown, bound for central and western Michigan.

The stories of fertile land and a pleasant climate aroused so much interest that "Michigan fever" struck many parts of the East. Hundreds of families hitched up and drove west, singing as they went.

> Come all you Yankee farmers who wish to change your lot,
> Who've spunk enough to travel beyond your native spot,
> And leave behind the village where Ma and Pa do stay,
> Come follow me and settle in Michigania —
> Yea! Yea! Yea! in Michigania!

Typical of the thousands of Americans who responded to "Michigan fever" was the Nowlin family. William Nowlin was a small boy when he arrived with his family in 1833. In later life he recalled how these pioneers traveled. His father bought eighty acres of land, sight unseen, two and a half miles from Detroit. In the spring of 1833, the family set out for Michigan from Putnam County, New York, with a school geography book as a guide. They went by wagon to Pough-keepsie, where they took a boat up the Hudson to meet an uncle who kept them over the winter in northern New York. The next spring the family packed everything they owned aboard a canal boat at Utica and took the Erie Canal to Buffalo. Here they boarded the steamer *Michigan*, one of the most famous passenger boats on the Lakes, and set out for Detroit. A storm on Lake Erie delayed the boat and fright-ened the youngsters, but the family finally reached Detroit, seasick and weary.

At Detroit, William's father hired a wagon, loaded his family and belongings into it, and drove out to their plot of land, near the present town of Dearborn. The Nowlins slept under the wagon and in a tent while the father and the boys put up a hastily built log cabin and later

a bark-covered house. They bought more land and prospered. They raised almost all their own food, living on bread, vegetables, and salt pork or beef. Mrs. Nowlin and the girls spun wool and flax to weave into cloth for clothes. Soon other families arrived. With the growth of the settlement, merchants, blacksmiths, cobblers, churches, schools came and in a few years, a town flourished. The story was repeated hundreds of times as the tide of settlement rolled across Michigan.

These immigrants from New York and New England, coming from established communities with experience in self-government, controlled Michigan's political, economic and intellectual life. The new constitution of the state contained many elements adapted from the laws of the Eastern states, and Michigan life reflected Eastern customs and manners. Many of the new towns, built with a village green faced by a church, resembled New England villages. The pioneers often named their settlements after ones they had left behind them — Clinton, Cambridge, Hudson, Canandaigua, New Boston, Palmyra, Rome Center, Ogden, Vermontville, Chelsea, and even Lansing, the new capital.

Lansing

But Michigan was destined to be much more than merely an exten-son of the East. During the first half of the nineteenth century a series of depressions, wars and revolutions against powerful governments led many people in Europe to look to the United States as a place where they might make a new start. All over Europe, people heard about the wide Michigan fields and forests, tried to pronounce the names of strange places like "Kalamazoo" and "Saginaw," and dreamed of moving to this land, fair, fertile, and free.

The idea of finding a new life in a new world drew immigrants to Michigan. Some of them were men who had never owned a foot of land, nor had their fathers, for centuries before them. Some were strong young men hoping to escape the endless round of cutting wood or digging potatoes for six cents a day. Some were old people, worn out with labor, who would never speak the language of the new coun-try. Some were bright-eyed children who would never know the grind-ing poverty of the old. The ships carried many cargoes to Michigan, but none so important as that stream of immigrants.

The first large group of foreigners to arrive were Germans, who came

Frankenmuth Bavarian children dance an old folk dance

in ever-greater boatloads. During the 1830's, one group settled near Ann Arbor and another at Westphalia, northeast of Lansing. Beginning in 1846, bands of German Lutherans, led by their ministers, began to settle in the Saginaw Valley, naming their towns Frankenmuth, Frankentrost, Frankenlust, and Frankenhuelf, after their home district of Franconia in Bavaria. Many of the Germans were farmers who came with sufficient money, raised from the sale of their farms at home, to buy good land. Some of them were skilled workers and professional men who settled in the cities. Before the Civil War, Detroit had German singing societies, turnvereins (social and physical exercise clubs), and a German theater.

Another group of immigrants who soon arrived in Michigan were the Dutch, who like the Plymouth Pilgrims came to escape religious persecution and to find better economic conditions. Holland had established a state church, of which some Dutchmen did not approve. They also suffered through a severe depression in the 1840's. The Reverend Albertus Van Raalte, a stubborn, godly man who refused to recognize the state church, left Holland with about fifty followers in 1846. He sailed to New York, and moved his flock to Detroit.

In the spring of 1847, Van Raalte and a party visited western Michigan. He found some excellent farmland at the mouth of the Black River, in Allegan County, purchased it, and brought his colony there later that year. Their Yankee neighbors showed the Dutch how to clear the land and build cabins. Their prosperous settlement (which they naturally named Holland) attracted other Hollanders. Another group settled Zeeland, others Vriesland, Drenthe, Graafchap, and Overisel, until about 40,000 Dutch had spread over the area. Their descendants are still the dominant social element in western Michigan, which bears the strong stamp of their language, customs and culture.

By the close of the nineteenth century, Michigan was a typically American melting pot of nationalities, all of them gradually being mixed and shaped into that new creature, the American. Finns and Danes came to work in the mines and on the ships with Cornishmen and Swedes. Poles came too. Some worked in the forests and mines, but most of them stayed in the cities. Hamtramck, a "Polish city" surrounded by Detroit, is the largest single concentration of Polish-

Americans in the United States. Detroit, nearly half of whose population is descended from foreign-born stock, has Italians, Hungarians, Mexicans, Greeks, Yugoslavs, Syrians, Bulgarians, and almost any other nationality one could name — including Eskimos, Afghans, and Malaysians, according to the latest census.

Negroes form one of the largest racial groups in Michigan, and one of the oldest. Since the Federal Ordinance of 1787 banished slavery from the Northwest Territory, of which Michigan was a part, few Negro slaves lived in Michigan. In 1837, when Michigan entered the Union, strong sentiment against slavery existed in the state. Many fugitive slaves, running away from their Southern masters, headed toward Michigan, knowing that antislavery sympathizers there would protect them and help them escape to Canada. The "Underground Railway," the escape route by which slaves fled North, had a number of "stations" in Michigan where antislavery men received the runaways and passed them on to the next stop. One route, known as the "Central Line," went through Cass County to Battle Creek, Marshall, Jackson, Dexter, Ypsilanti, and on to Detroit. Another line ran from Toledo to Adrian, Tecumseh, Ypsilanti, and then to Detroit or Port Huron. The "stations" were usually farmhouses where the runaways could be fed and hidden — sometimes in secret basement or attic rooms — located every fifteen to twenty miles along the route. No one knows how many Negro slaves passed through Michigan to freedom, but Erastus Hussey, a Quaker who lived at Battle Creek, was said to have helped more than a thousand of them.

Many of these fugitive Negroes stayed in Michigan. In Calvin Township, near Cassopolis, seventy-five percent of the population is descended from former slaves, making it the oldest Negro community in the state, and one of the oldest in the entire Midwest.

The great migration of Negro population to Michigan came during and after the two World Wars. The demand for labor in Michigan's factories drew thousands of Negroes to the state, where they found opportunities for employment not available to them in the South. The majority of these Negroes came to the industrialized cities, where wartime production was at its highest. Negroes produced much of the armament and munitions that poured out of the Detroit-Flint-Pontiac area during the war. Over the years Michigan's Negro population has played an important role in the state's industrial, professional and political life. Detroit has more Negro-owned and Negro-controlled businesses than any other large city. It has contributed Negro-citizens to the nation as different as the universally respected athlete Joe Louis and Otis Smith, Justice of the Michigan Supreme Court, who holds one of the highest elective offices of any Negro in the country.

Michigan, then, is people: a mixture of nationalities and races and languages that have combined over many years to produce Americans. It has always been so, since the Frenchman and the Indian lived side by side in the fur-trade post with the Scottish merchant, since the Italian and the Finn went down into the mines with the Cornishman, since the Hungarian and the Syrian went to work with the Negro on the automobile assembly line.

Chapter 9

Highlights of the Past

The history of any one of the United States is complex. Michigan is no exception. Its early history is part of France's attempt to found a North American empire. Its middle years belong to England's eighteenth-century drive to the west. Its American history is part of the story of how the great Northwest Territory, won from the English in the Revolution, emerged into statehood. Michigan's past lies under these three flags — one might even say four. In 1781, Spanish raiders once claimed Fort St. Joseph, near Niles, for a few days. And it is a long past, for it should not be forgotten that the French had already discovered Michigan when the little English colonies at Plymouth and Jamestown were struggling to keep a foothold on the Atlantic coast, seven hundred miles to the east.

Three and a half centuries of Michigan history cannot be briefly summarized. But certain events, chosen from over the years, provide

Historic Lansing state capitol

highlights worth noting. One of the most important is Michigan's discovery.

Samuel de Champlain, the adventurous governor of New France who founded Quebec in 1608, knew where the Michigan country was. He thought it might lie at the edge of something important — a new route to China, a land of fabulous cities and gold such as the Spanish had found in South America, a forest wilderness teeming with valuable furs. The challenge of the unknown lured Champlain up the St. Lawrence, into the Ottawa river, and finally in 1615 to the shores of Lake Huron.

But it was not Champlain who first saw the land that became Michigan. It was Étienne Brûle, a young French woodsman who had been sent by Champlain to live with the Huron Indians near Lake Simcoe in Canada and find out what he could about the country. Brûle heard stories of good game lands and great lakes to the west. About the winter of 1619, he traveled with a Huron party to the rapids of the St. Mary's river at the Sault. Three years later Brûle returned, paddled out into Lake Superior itself, explored its south shore, and brought back a nugget of copper, showing that he may have gone as far as the Marquette country.

Young Brûle almost certainly was the first European to see Michigan. His reports to Champlain helped map the routes for the expanding fur trade on which New France's prosperity depended, and encouraged later explorers, like Jean Nicolet, to push on farther west. The Lower Peninsula of Michigan remained relatively unexplored for thirty years or more after Brûle's trip, for there was danger there from hostile Iroquois who controlled the Ohio region. Curiously enough the Upper Peninsula, which later became part of Michigan almost by accident, was the first to be explored, mapped, and settled. And the man who was most responsible for finding it, Samuel de Champlain, never saw it himself.

Antoine de la Mothe Cadillac, who arrived in Canada in 1683, was an adventurous, hard-driving man much like Samuel de Champlain. Cadillac came to New France to find wealth, land and power. In 1694, Governor Frontenac, who liked him, sent Cadillac to command Fort

Buade, the most important French post in the Mackinac country. Cadillac was an excellent soldier and administrator. However, he did not get along well with the powerful Jesuit fathers at Mackinac, and when King Louis XIV closed the region to traders, Cadillac returned to Quebec, a wealthy man but not wealthy enough to be satisfied.

In 1666, the young Jesuit priest, Father Jacques Marquette, was sent from France to Sault Ste. Marie and later to St. Ignace, where the Jesuits had recently established missions to serve the Indians in the eastern half of the Michigan peninsula.

The Chippewa Indians told Father Marquette about a great river called the Miss-sipi and he was determined to find it. Jean Talon, the governor at Quebec, wanted to find it, too. He chose Louis Joliet to head the expedition and Joliet selected Father Marquette to go with him in the spring of 1673. Together with five other men, they undertook one of the great exploring journeys in American history. They penetrated into the heart of the Continent, and brought out detailed information concerning the greatest river and the richest wilderness in North America — and the conviction that the Mississippi River flowed into neither the Atlantic Ocean nor the Pacific Ocean, but the Gulf of Mexico.

Father Marquette was never to return to St. Ignace. On the journey back, he died somewhere near the mouth of the river in southern Michigan which today bears his name.

At Quebec Cadillac thought of a new plan, to establish a military and trading post at the lower end of Lake Huron, at the straits called "Le Detroit" that lay between Lake St. Clair and Lake Erie. He knew from studying the maps that this was a strategic military and commercial point, for it not only controlled the Erie-Huron waterway but might serve to block English expansion into the Great Lakes area. If the King would grant him land at the Straits of Mackinac, he would fill it with settlers, establish a trading post and build a fort, thereby giving France an important military position and at the same time filling his own pockets by trade. What Cadillac had in mind was the creation of a huge feudal estate, larger than that possessed by any nobleman in France, with himself as military commander, trader and authority

over hundreds of fertile farms. Antoine de la Mothe Cadillac thought in large terms.

Both Count Pontchartrain, the King's colonial minister, and the King were convinced by Cadillac's persuasiveness. But by the time he was ready to leave for Michigan his friend Frontenac was dead and New France bubbled with political plots. Nevertheless, Cadillac left Quebec City in June, 1701, with fifty soldiers, two priests, a hundred Indians, and his nine-year-old son, bound for Le Detroit. On July 24 he chose a spot on the river (at the foot of what is now Woodward Avenue) and built a log fort which he named Fort Pontchartrain du Detroit. It was a crude affair, but by the end of summer the party had constructed a wall of logs two hundred feet square, enclosing a chapel, a barracks, and some log huts. It was still a military post. But when Madame Cadillac and Madame Tonty (the wife of Cadillac's second

Marquette and Joliet

in command) arrived in the late fall with household goods and children, the city of Detroit may properly be said to have begun.

Cadillac's settlement grew and prospered. He treated the Indians well, developed a thriving trade, and sent glowing reports to Quebec. Settlers came (their names, Beaubien, Aubin, Chene, and others, still mark Detroit streets) and the place took on the appearance of a community. But at Quebec City the political pot was at full boil. Plenty of men wanted Cadillac's profitable post at Detroit, and he had the support neither of the new governor nor of the Jesuits who remembered their clashes with him at Fort Buade. Charges were made against him. He was tried and cleared of blame in 1704; and after that he was constantly on the defensive. In 1710 his rivals won. He was appointed Governor of Louisiana, actually a more important post, but one that removed him permanently from Detroit. As soon as he left, others seized his land, and after King Louis' death the colonial officers in Paris stripped him even of his title to it. His successors governed Detroit badly while Cadillac, a defeated and disappointed man, returned to France to die in 1730. Little remains in Detroit of his great plan except the name given the city by the proud, ambitious soldier who first chose the spot where the city stands.

As fate would have it, Cadillac's dream of splendor along the straits of Detroit was doomed to failure in any event. France soon surrendered her North American possessions to England, and thirty years after Cadillac's death, on November 29, 1760, Major Robert Rogers ran up the British flag in Detroit in the name of his king. But British rule did not last. Sixteen years later, the Continental Congress, meeting at Philadelphia, declared its independence of Great Britain. In 1783, by the Treaty of Paris that closed the Revolution, the United States took title to all the Northwest.

Legally, Michigan belonged to the new United States. In practical terms, there was a good deal of doubt. The British simply refused to withdraw their soldiers, hoping among other things that by remaining in the Northwest territories, somehow England might discourage the new American government from actually taking possession.

To complicate matters, it was not at all clear who really owned the Northwest country. Massachusetts, Connecticut, New York and Virginia all claimed parts of Michigan. Not until 1786, when these states surrendered their claims, did the national government really own the Northwest. In 1787 Congress passed the Northwest Ordinance, providing methods by which this great new expanse could be settled, governed and eventually formed into states. As far as Michigan was concerned, the Ordinance had little immediate effect. The British army still held Detroit and hostile Indian tribes threatened American settlements through the whole region.

When General "Mad Anthony" Wayne soundly defeated Chief Blue Jacket and his Indians at the Battle of Fallen Timbers (near Toledo) in 1796, the British reluctantly withdrew from Detroit and American forces finally marched in. Even then, only a few American settlers lived in Michigan, which was simply an undeveloped part of the Northwest Territory. In 1800, officials in Washington included half of Michigan in Indiana Territory. In 1805, when Ohio attained statehood, they made Michigan a separate territory, attached half the Upper Peninsula to it, and located its capital at Detroit.

Michigan's most difficult period began. Though the British were gone, their agents and traders, working from Canada, plotted against the American government and stirred up the Indians. The federal government was having trouble defending its western frontier, and sparsely populated Michigan was too far from Washington for the national government to pay much attention to it. Furthermore, the United States and Britain were close to war. When hostilities did break out in 1812, Washington officials, by some incredible blundering, failed to notify the frontier outposts. The British forces near Mackinac, hearing that war was declared, simply walked into the fort and captured it. The American commander at Detroit, General William Hull, heard about the declaration of war by accident. On August 16, 1812, he surrendered the city in panic to a much smaller British force. Michigan and most of the Great Lakes area fell like a ripe plum into British hands.

It took many months for the Americans to win it back. General William Harrison, an experienced frontier fighter, organized an army and worked his way slowly up through Indiana and Ohio, training his soldiers as he went. By the winter of 1813 his troops rested in the Maumee country, near Fallen Timbers. At the same time a young American naval captain, Oliver Hazard Perry, arrived at Lake Erie. He was to build a fleet in order to take control of the lakes away from the British who were based at Amherstburg and Fort Malden, near Detroit on the Canadian side. Perry, who had nine small ships and a motley crew of soldiers, sailors and civilians, engaged the British fleet on September 10, 1813, near Put-in-Bay, a small island almost due south of Detroit. After a bloody all-day battle Perry sent Harrison his famous message, "We have met the enemy and they are ours."

Perry's victory opened the Lake route to Detroit, and Harrison swiftly moved his army by ship toward the British stronghold at Fort Malden. British General Henry Procter decided to abandon Detroit and retreat toward Toronto. With him went the Indian army commanded by Tecumseh, the powerful Shawnee chieftain who hated

Americans bitterly and who was the most feared of the Indian leaders. But they could not move fast enough. Harrison's advance guard once more raised the American flag over Detroit while his main army caught Procter's force at the Thames River, near the present town of Thamesville, Ontario, on October 5. Tecumseh's Indians fought savagely. Tecumseh himself was killed, and six hundred British were taken prisoner. General Lewis Cass of Harrison's army, left in command of Detroit, shortly received word that he had been appointed governor of Michigan Territory, a post he held for the next eighteen years.

Perry's and Harrison's victories marked the end of British and Indian threats to Michigan's security. Settlers streamed in to occupy the rich lands and forests that stretched across southern Michigan. When young Stevens T. Mason took over the direction of territorial affairs in 1834, most territorial leaders thought it was time that Michigan became a state. A census showed 85,000 people in Michigan, more than enough to warrant admission to the Union under the terms of the Northwest Ordinance. In 1835 a convention met in Detroit to write a constitution for statehood. The voters approved it that same year, and elected Mason governor.

Prospects for early statehood looked encouraging, except for the situation in Ohio. Ohio, already a state and much more influential than Michigan, wanted to make absolutely sure that if Michigan entered the Union, it did so without the so-called "Toledo Strip," the ownership of which was at the moment being hotly contested. At the same time, the Southerners in Congress opposed Michigan's entry as a free state since it would upset the carefully guarded balance of power between slave and free states. The argument dragged on in Washington until finally the politicians arranged a compromise. If Michigan ceded the disputed strip to Ohio, it could have all the Upper Peninsula. If Arkansas, a slave territory, could be admitted at the same time, Michigan's petition for statehood would have Southern support. Since Michigan had no power to negotiate the terms, Mason and his men could do little but agree.

Back in Michigan, however, many did not. Tempers flared and feelings ran high. The territorial convention, meeting in Ann Arbor in 1836, debated the compromise for four days and flatly rejected it with a blast against both Ohio and Congress. But other forces were at work. Political appointments to the new state offices had already been promised, public lands were about to be put up for sale, and — most convincing of all — the federal treasury was about to distribute portions of its surplus to states, not territories.

Although they had doubtful authority to do so, the officials of the Democratic party (Mason's party) called another convention of carefully chosen delegates in December of 1836 (called the "frostbitten convention" because of the weather), which accepted the compromise quickly and so notified Congress. The Senate swiftly ratified Michigan's entry on January 26, 1837, and President Jackson signed the bill into law, placing the twenty-sixth star in the field of the American flag. There were many who disagreed with the compromise and who claimed that the convention was not only frostbitten but illegal.

Statehood marked the opening of a period of unprecedented growth and prosperity for Michigan. Since it became a state under the reign of President Andrew Jackson, Michigan generally favored Jackson's Democratic party over the Whigs, the other major party of the time. The introduction of the slavery question into politics, however, at the same time as Michigan's admission, soon changed the complexion of the state's politics, as it did throughout the Northwest. The passage of the national Fugitive Slave Law in 1850, which provided for the return of runaway slaves, seemed to turn Michiganders into slave-catchers. The law raised political passions to a white heat.

Neither the Democratic nor the Whig party seemed willing to take a stand against slavery. The issue cut across party lines in Michigan, and divided friends and families. When the Kansas-Nebraska Act of 1854 was passed by Congress, apparently opening up the western territories to slavery, opponents of the system decided the time had come for decision. Antislavery men of both parties agreed to hold a joint meeting at which, if it seemed practical, they might form a new political party that was unquestionably against slavery.

They selected Jackson as the site of the meeting, and on July 6, 1854, five thousand delegates descended on the town. Since no hall in Jackson was large enough to hold so many, the convention assembled outdoors in a grove of spreading oak trees. There were speeches, resolutions and little debate, for the delegates knew why they had come. The meeting demanded that Congress repeal the fugitive-slave laws, reconsider the Kansas-Nebraska Act, and rule against the admission of slavery into the new territories. It also founded a new party, calling it "Republican," a name intended to affirm the delegates' faith in the unity of the Republic.

Angry antislavery men were meeting elsewhere in the country in 1854, but the Jackson assembly was the first such statewide meeting, the first to adopt a platform and the first to nominate a full state ticket of candidates under the new party name. What began at Jackson swept across the nation. Out of the crucial debate over the issues of slavery and union a new political force was born. Abraham Lincoln came to Michigan to speak to the party's convention. Six years later the movement that started under the trees that day at Jackson put

him in the White House. A cairn of stones marks the spot today, with a bronze plate that reads, "Here under the oaks, July 6, 1854, was born the Republican Party, destined in the throes of civil strife to abolish slavery, vindicate Democracy, and perpetuate the Union."

History is often made by small decisions. Things we accept today without question sometimes might not exist, had something long ago turned out differently. An example is the Kalamazoo School case of 1874, which settled for Michigan — and for most of the United States — whether or not there would be public high schools. Michigan's constitution provided for a system of "common schools," that is, schools which gave a minimum education in reading, writing and arithmetic. Admittedly many of these were not good schools. They were no more than one-room log huts where underpaid teachers taught classes for as little as three months of the year. But as Michigan's population

Old one-room schoolhouse

increased after the Civil War, its schools expanded and improved. In 1860 the legislature passed a new law allowing school districts to collect taxes for support of public high schools. This was an important step, for as a rule many schools stopped at the eighth grade. If a boy or girl wanted to continue, their parents had to pay tuition at a private academy.

The law raised a number of questions. How far should public support for education go? At what point did the responsibility of the state end, and that of parents begin? Did the state have the right to tax people without children for the education of others? Was not a "common school" education enough? Actually, all these questions revolved about the issue of whether or not the state ought to provide tax-supported, free public education, and if so, how much of it. There were those in Michigan and elsewhere who believed that the increase in such tax-supported schools had gone far enough.

In 1873 three citizens of Kalamazoo filed a request in court to prevent the township treasurer from collecting taxes to support a new high school, and to prevent the school board from spending tax money for it. The 1869 law, the petition claimed, was unconstitutional. The complaint lost in Circuit Court, but its framers appealed it to the State Supreme Court. Every parent and schoolteacher knew it was an important case, for on its resolution rested the fate of every free public high school in the state.

In July of 1874 Justice Thomas Cooley, summarizing the unanimous opinion of the Court, refused to overturn the lower court's decision. There were no qualifications, he concluded, on the right of the state to establish schools if the voters desired, no end to the extent of the education those schools might offer, and no restrictions on what these schools might teach if needed. The decision reached far beyond Michigan. It implied the right of a state to establish a complete education system, from primary grades through university, at public expense. It came at the right time, too, for public high schools were springing up in the Midwestern states in great numbers. Had the case been settled differently, it seems doubtful that there would be high schools as we have them today, or perhaps state universities. Fortunately for later generations of American students, the Kalamazoo case helped to make today's public education possible.

Probably the most decisive change in Michigan's economic history came with its conversion to the automobile manufacturing center of the world, a change accomplished swiftly in the space of a single generation.

The phenomenal growth of the automobile industry in Michigan brought thousands of workers into the state, particularly the industrial cities. Since the mass-production methods of automobile manufacture were highly automated, the great majority of these workers — ninety-eight percent, in fact — needed no particular skills. Existing labor unions were interested chiefly in recruiting craftsmen, not laborers. During the 1930's, in the midst of the Depression, a movement to organize unskilled workers in unions began in a number of such mass-production industries. The Congress of Industrial Organizations, a new labor body, came into being. The most important member of this group, so far as Michigan was concerned, was the United Automobile Workers, the UAW.

By 1936 the UAW claimed nearly a half million members in Michigan. Its struggle with the companies to gain recognition as the bargaining agent for workers in the industry was a stormy one. Over the next five years, Flint, Lansing, Pontiac, and Detroit were the scenes of hard-fought contests between labor and management. In 1940 and 1941, however, elections held by the National Labor Relations Board established the UAW as the official representative of the auto workers. Since that time management and labor within the industry have learned to work together for mutual benefit. Over the past quarter-century the UAW, under the leadership of Walter Reuther, who became its president in 1946, has served as a pioneer in the field of modern labor relations, and occupies a leading position in Michigan's political and economic life.

Because Michigan was known as "the automobile state," the fact that it was impossible to drive its length, from Detroit to Copper Harbor, bothered Michiganders. The barrier between Michigan's two peninsulas, of course, was four miles of blue water, the Straits of Mackinac, that had separated them since the close of the Ice Age. Indians crossed the Straits in canoes or on the ice in winter; traders and settlers used *bateaux* and flatboats. But the crossing in any season could be dangerous, and no one will ever know the toll of lives and goods taken by the Straits over the centuries.

Beginning in the 1880's, steam ferries hauled railroad cars from Mackinaw City to St. Ignace and back. In 1923 the State Highway Department established a ferry service for automobiles. Thousands of

Michigan motorists recall the white, double-ended ferry boats with their musical whistles that shuttled back and forth ten times daily, carrying waiting autos across the sparkling waters.

The Straits always presented a challenge. That stretch of open water seemed to demand a bridge to remedy nature's ancient division of two peninsulas. Many talked about it, and many dismissed it as an idle dream. In 1934 the legislature finally appointed the Mackinac Bridge Authority to investigate the possibility of constructing a bridge. It took twenty years to reach a decision, but in 1954 the first

"Big Mac"

piledriver hammered at the floor of the Straits and "Big Mac" began to take shape. On May 17, 1957, after workmen fitted the last piece of steel into place, one could walk across the Straits for the first time in history. The Mackinac Bridge not only made Michigan geographically one state, but brought Canada and the East closer to the Great Lakes country.

Designed by David Steinman, one of America's famous bridge builders, the Mackinac Bridge is one of the most amazing structures of the world. A suspension bridge, its center span hangs from two tremendous towers, each 552 feet high, whose foundations reach two hundred feet below the surface of the water to bedrock. It can be described only in superlatives. One million tons of steel and concrete went into the making of it; 10,000 men built it, working from 85,000 blueprints; its suspension cables, each made of 12,000 steel wires woven together, would reach twice around the world. The center span measures 3,800 feet; the overall length is nearly five miles. Constructed by two separate crews, one to build the foundation and another the superstructure, the bridge was put together from prefabricated steel parts which, when fitted together, matched to the fraction of an inch.

Today, then, the motorist can speed across the Straits, a hundred feet over the water, on the same journey that took the Frenchman with his boatload of furs a full day. Jean Nicolet, who first saw the Straits in 1634, might rub his eyes at the sight. But then again it seems likely that he might understand. He, too, was an adventurer, answering the challenge of the untried and unknown. Of this, the spirit that made Michigan what it is today, the Big Bridge stands as a modern symbol.

Michigan Profile
The Wolverine State

GENERAL

Statehood   January 26, 1837; twenty-sixth state to join the Union
Area   58,216 square miles; thirty-second ranking state
Population   8,098,000 (1964); seventh-ranking state
Capital   Lansing
Motto   *Si quaeris peninsulam amoenam, circumspice*
    If you seek a pleasant peninsula, look about you
Flower   Apple blossom
Bird   Robin
Tree   White pine
Song   "Michigan, My Michigan" (unofficial)

PHYSICAL CHARACTERISTICS
Boundaries

North   Lake Superior and Lake Huron, with Canada opposite
East   Lake Erie, Lake Huron and Ontario, Canada
South   Indiana and Ohio (Lower Peninsula); Wisconsin and Lake Michigan (Upper Peninsula)
West   Lake Michigan with Wisconsin and Illinois opposite

Greatest width   Upper Peninsula: 334 miles east to west
    Lower Peninsula: 200 miles east to west
Greatest length   Upper Peninsula: 215 miles north to south
    Lower Peninsula: 286 miles north to south
Highest point   1,980 feet above sea level in Baraga County
Lowest point   572 feet above sea level along Lake Erie

Climate

Cold and snowy winters and mild summers. Adequate rainfall. Highest recorded temperature: 112°. Lowest recorded temperature: −51°.

Principal cities

Detroit: 1,670,144
Flint: 196,940
Grand Rapids: 177,313
Dearborn: 112,007
Lansing: 107,807

Saginaw: 98,265
Pontiac: 82,233
Kalamazoo: 82,089
Bay City: 53,604
Jackson: 50,720

Principal mountains

Copper Range
Gogebic Range
Huron Mountains

Menominee Range
Porcupine Mountains

Principal rivers

Au Sable
Detroit
Grand
Kalamazoo
Manistee

Manistique
Muskegon
Saginaw
St. Clair
St. Marys

Principal lakes

Burt
Charlevoix
Crystal
Gogebic
Houghton

Manistique
Mullet
Portage
Torch

LEADING PRODUCTS

Manufacturing

Motor vehicles and parts, cereal preparations, machine tools, hardware, steel springs, furniture, padding and upholstering, industrial patterns, nonferrous castings, industrial leather belts, paperboard mills, gray-iron foundries, paper, chemicals, lumber, and missiles

Agriculture

Tart cherries, peaches, plums, apples, grapes, sweet cherries, cucumbers, blueberries, mint. Dry beans, corn, winter wheat, sugar beets, soybeans, potatoes, oats, celery. Livestock and dairy products

Minerals

Iron ore, copper, cement, petroleum, sand and gravel, stone, salt, magnesium, limestone, natural gas, sandstone

Fishing

Herring, perch, pickerel, pike, smelt, trout, whitefish

Tourism

Second-ranking industry in Michigan
Longest freshwater shoreline facing the four Great Lakes; water sports, festivals, winter carnivals, trout fishing, hunting
One national park, five national forests
sixty-five state parks, twenty-five state forests

GOVERNMENT

United States Congress

Senators: 2
Representatives: 18

State Legislature

Senators: 20
Representatives: 34

Counties in Michigan: 110

HISTORY

1618   The Michigan region was visited by Etienne Brule, a French explorer.

1634   Jean Nicolet came to the region.

1668   Father Jacques Marquette, a French missionary and explorer, founded the first permanent settlement at Sault Ste. Marie.

1671   Father Marquette founded a mission among the Hurons at Michilimackinac.

1679   René de la Salle built a fort at the mouth of the St. Joseph.

1701   Antoine Cadillac founded Detroit.

1763   Uprising under Chief Pontiac; Detroit was besieged for five months. The British took possession of Michigan after the French and Indian War.

1783   Great Britain ceded Michigan to the United States.

1787   Michigan became part of the Northwest Territory.

1794   General Anthony Wayne defeated the Indians and the British at the Battle of Fallen Timbers.

1796   Detroit and Mackinac finally surrendered to the United States and the British completely withdrew from Michigan.

1805   The Michigan Territory was organized.

1812   The British recaptured Detroit and Fort Mackinac.

1813   Commodore Oliver H. Perry defeated British ships on Lake Erie. Lewis Cass became territorial governor.

1818   The first steamboat, *Walk-in-Water*, appeared at Detroit.

1825 The Erie Canal opened.

1835 Stevens T. Mason became the first state governor.

1837 Michigan became the twenty-sixth state on January 26th.

1842 Michigan obtained Isle Royale and Keweenaw in the Upper Peninsula from the Indians — copper country.

1845 Michigan's first copper mine opened at Copper Harbor.

1846 Michigan's iron industry began near Negaunee.

1847 Lansing became the state capital.

1852 The Michigan Central Railroad was completed to Chicago.

1854 The Republican party was organized at Jackson.

1855 The Soo Canal was completed at Sault Ste. Marie.

1865 The Fourth Michigan Cavalry captured President Jefferson Davis of the Confederacy, near Irwinville, Georgia.

1870 Michigan was the leading lumber-producing state.

1899 Michigan's first automobile factory was established in Detroit by Ransom E. Olds.

1909 Michigan was the first state to construct a concrete highway.

1914 The Ford Motor Company set a wage precedent by establishing the minimum daily wage of $5.

1917–18 During World War I, Michigan factories produced airplanes, tanks and other war materials.

1920's More and improved roads were built. The automobile industry continued to grow and develop.

1935 The United Auto Workers Union was begun by Michigan workers.

1942–45 Michigan automobile industry converted to war production during World War II.

1954 The state's mining industry began processing low-grade ore. New copper mines were opened.

1955 One of the largest blast furnaces in the world went into operation near Detroit.

1957 The Straits of Mackinac Bridge was opened to traffic between Mackinac City and St. Ignace.

1962 The International Bridge was opened at Sault Ste. Marie.

1964 Michigan's new constitution went into effect.

GOVERNORS

Stevens T. Mason	1835–1840	Edwin B. Winans	1891–1893
Edward Mundy	1838	John T. Rich	1893–1897
William Woodbridge	1840–1841	Hazen S. Pingree	1897–1901
James W. Gordon	1841–1842	Aaron T. Bliss	1901–1905
John S. Barry	1842–1846	Fred M. Warner	1905–1911
Alpheus Felch	1846–1847	Chase S. Osborn	1911–1913
William L. Greenly	1847–1848	Woodbridge N. Ferris	1913–1917
Epaphroditus Ransom	1848–1850	Albert E. Sleeper	1917–1921
John S. Barry	1850–1851	Alexander J. Groesbeck	1921–1927
Robert McClelland	1851–1853	Frederick W. Green	1927–1931
Andrew Parsons	1853–1855	Wilbur M. Brucker	1931–1933
Kinsley S. Bingham	1855–1859	William A. Comstock	1933–1935
Moses Wisner	1859–1861	Frank D. Fitzgerald	1935–1937
Austin Blair	1861–1865	Frank Murphy	1937–1938
Henry H. Crapo	1865–1869	Frank D. Fitzgerald	1939
Henry P. Baldwin	1869–1873	Luren D. Dickinson	1939–1941
John J. Bagley	1873–1877	Murray D. van Wagoner	1941–1943
Charles M. Croswell	1877–1881	Harry F. Kelly	1943–1947
David H. Jerome	1881–1883	Kim Sigler	1947–1949
Josiah W. Begole	1883–1885	G. Mennen Williams	1949–1961
Russell A. Alger	1885–1887	John B. Swainson	1961–1963
Cyrus G. Luce	1887–1891	George Romney	1963–

PEOPLE AND MICHIGAN

Ralph Bunche

Antoine Cadillac

Will Carleton

Lewis Cass

Bruce Catton

Robert Caveliar

Zachariah Chandler

Walter P. Chrysler

Charles E. Coughlin

James Couzens

Harlow H. Curtice

James O. Curwood

W. C. Durant

Dodge brothers

Woodbridge N. Ferris

Henry Ford

Edgar A. Guest

Douglass Houghton

J. H. Hudson

George M. Humphrey

Louis Joliet

William K. Kellogg

S. S. Kresge

Ring Lardner

Henry Leland

Charles Lindbergh

Father Jacques Marquette

Stevens T. Mason

Frank Murphy

Ransom E. Olds

Oliver H. Perry

C. W. Post

Walter Reuther

Gabriel Richard

George Romney

René de la Salle

Arthur Vandenburg

Anthony Wayne

G. Mennen Williams

PRONUNCIATION GUIDE

Algonquin	Al *gong* kwin	Marquette	Mar *ket*
Allegan	*Al* ih gan	Mascoutin	Mas *coo* tin
Alpena	Al *pee* na	Menominee	Me *nom* a nee
Antrim	*An* trim	Michilimackinac	*Mish* ih li *mak* i naw
Au Sable	Oh *Sah* ble	Muskegon	Mus *kee* gan
Brule	Brool	Navaho	Nah va *hoe*
		Negaunee	Ni *gaw* nee
Cadillac	*Kad* ih lak	Newaygo	Nee *way* go
Calumet	*Kal* u met	Nicolet	Nee ko *lay*
Canandaigua	Kan n *day* gwa		
Cassopolis	Kah *sop* a lis	Ojibwa	O *jib* wah
Champlain	Sham *plane*	Okimos	O *kee* mos
Charlevoix	*Shar* la voy	Ontonagon	On tuh *naw* gun
Cheboygan	Shi *boy* gan	Oscoda	Os *ko* da
Chippewa	*Chip* eh wah	Otsego	Ot *see* go
coureurs de bois	coo rurr de bwa	Ottawa	*Ot* ah wa
		Overisel	Over *eye* sel
Drenthe	*Dren* ta		
Duluth	Da *looth*	Palmyra	Pal *my* ra
		Pontiac	*Pon* tee ak
Escanaba	Es ka *naw* ba	Pottawattomi	Pot a *wot* a mee
Franconia	Fran *ko* nee a	Poughkeepsie	Pah *kip* see
Frankfort	*Frang* furt		
		Saginaw	*Sag* i naw
Gitche Manido	*Git* chee Man *ee* doe	Sauks	Soks
Gitche Manito	*Git* chee Man *ee* toe	Sault Ste. Marie	Soo Sant *May* ree
Gogebic	Go *gee* bik	Seney	*See* nee
Graafchap		Shawnee	*Shaw* nee
Grand Marais	Grand Mah *ray*	Simcoe	*Sim* koe
		St. Ignace	St. *Ig* nus
Hamtramck	Ham *tram* ik		
		Tecumseh	Ta *kum* sah
Iroquois	*Ir* ah kwoi	Toivola	Toy *voe* la
Ishpeming	*Ish* pa ming	Topinabee	*Ta* pun a bee
		Turnverein	*toorn* fehr ine
Joliet	*Jo* lee et		
		Vandalia	Van *day* lee ah
Kalamazoo	Kal ah mah *zoo*	voyageur	voy a *zher*
Keweenaw	*Kee* wi naw	Vreisland	*Vrees* land
Lac Sainte Claire	Lak sant Clare	Wauseon	*Waw* see on
		Wenibojo	When e *bo* jo
Mackinac	Mak i naw	Wyandot	*Wy* n dot
Manabozho	Ma na *boes* o		
Manabush	*Ma* na bush	Ypsilanti	Ip si *lan* tee
Manistee	Man is *tee*		
Manistique	Man is *teek*	Zeeland	*Zee* land
Manitoulin	Man i *too* lin		

INDEX

123

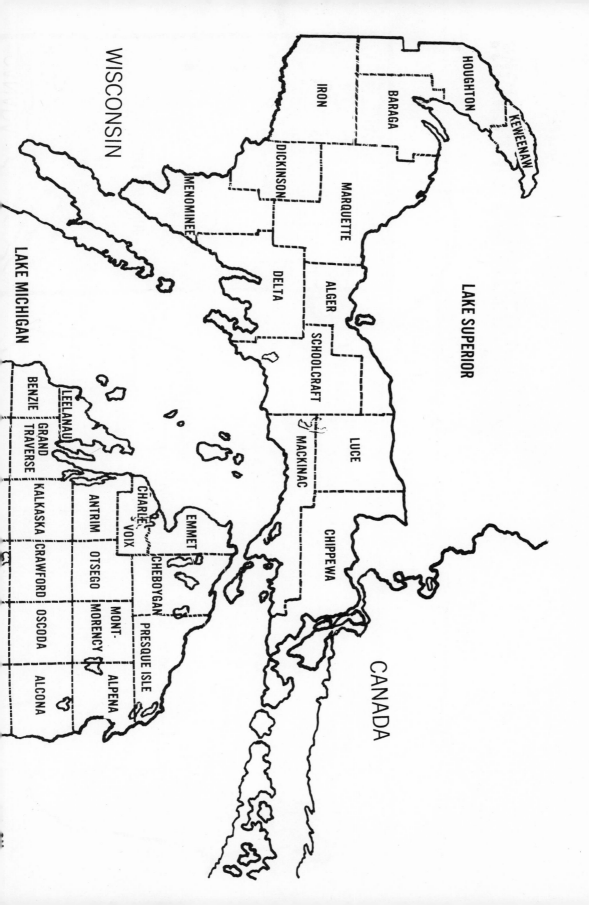

STATES OF THE NATION

The "States of the Nation" books provide young readers with an exciting, current profile of each state in the Union.

Within the borders of a state, one finds an individual place that has developed and grown historically, geographically and culturally to become shaped and molded to what it is today. These books explore the character and special qualities of the state, its unique features, and who and what contributed to its making.

To present a vivid, fresh portrayal of each state demanded a thoughtful selection of authors. We have chosen writers who know their state personally, who have a special feeling for it, and who write about it with liveliness, enthusiasm and authority. Each book in the series has had a careful, step-by-step check with a leading state consultant. An extensive reference section at the back of each book includes basic facts and statistics, a chronological synopsis of history, governors and famous people, a pronunciation guide, and a comprehensive index.

MICHIGAN
by Russel B. Nye

OREGON
by Iris Noble

VIRGINIA
by Michael Frome

The Author

Russel B. Nye lives in East Lansing, Michigan. He is a professor of English at Michigan State University.

Professor Nye was born and reared in the Midwest where he has always lived, with the exception of one year spent in New York. Born in Wisconsin, he spent his summers as a youth in Michigan. He has traveled extensively through the state and has lived in both the Upper and the Lower Peninsula. For the past twenty-six years, he has made his home in Michigan with his family. He has one son.

Professor Nye has written sixteen books in the fields of American literature and American history. His biography, *George Bancroft: Brahmin Rebel*, was awarded the Pulitzer Prize for biography in 1945.

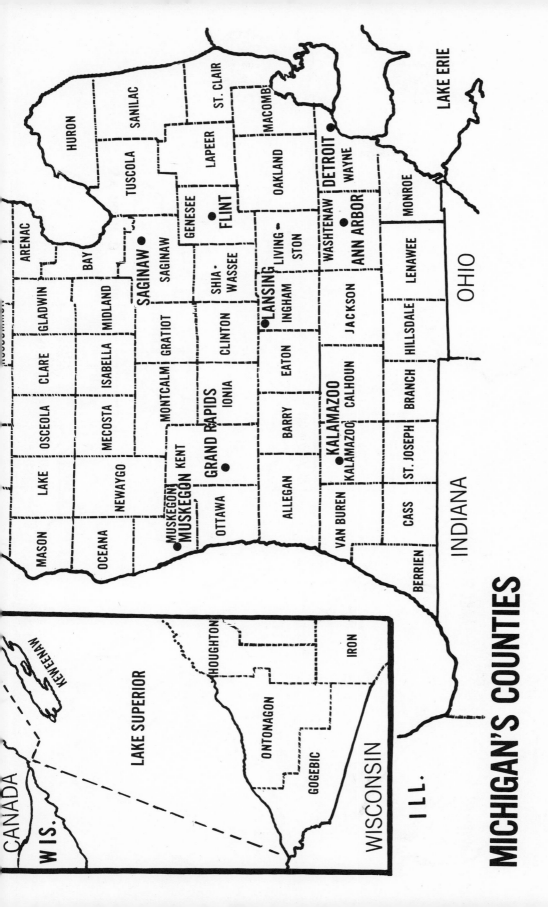

MICHIGAN'S COUNTIES